We Interrupt This Programme...

WE INTERRUPT THIS PROGRAMME...

20 NEWS STORIES THAT MARKED THE CENTURY

Peter Barnard

Foreword by John Humphrys

Published by BBC Worldwide Limited,
Woodlands, 80 Wood Lane, London W12 0TT

First published in 1999
© Peter Barnard 1999
The moral right of the author has been asserted

ISBN 0 563 55137 2

The texts of Winston Churchill's wartime speeches
on pages 47 and 48 are reproduced with permission
of Curtis Brown Ltd, London, on behalf of the Estate
of Sir Winston S. Churchill. Copyright Winston
S. Churchill.

Commissioning Editors: Sue Kerr and Anna Ottewill
Project Editor: Julian Flanders
Art Editor: Lisa Pettibone
Designer: Paul Welti
CD Researcher and Compiler: Mark Jones
Picture Researcher: Miriam Hyman

Set in Gill Sans Light
Printed and bound in France by Imprimerie Pollina s.a.
Jacket printed in France by Imprimerie Pollina s.a..

Picture Credits:
BBC 2, 7, 14, 47, 48, 52, 54;
Camera Press 12, 20, 38, 39, 49, 50, 62, 74, 75, 90, 94,
134, 148, 151, 152, 155, 158, 166, 177, 181, 189, 215,
217; 220
Corbis 24, 27, 28, 31, 37, 43, 68, 97, 146, 179;
Genesis Space Photo Library 109, 111, 113, 116, 117;
Hulton Getty 10, 18,19, 33, 34, 44, 45, 57, 61, 64, 65,
66, 71, 79, 81, 82, 87, 92, 93, 96, 119, 130, 139, 140,
142, 145, 150, 180, 187, 192;
Katz 103, 196, 199, 200, 203, 204, 205, 218;
Katz/Time Life 16, 46, 58, 89;
Magnum 106, 219;
Manchester United Museum and Tour Centre 84, 85;
Mirror Syndication 197;
NASA 9, 110, 114, 115;
PA News 5, 83, 99, 137, 157, 161, 162, 163, 165, 169,
172, 174, 175, 184, 190, 209;
Popperfoto 23, 80, 100, 101, 104, 122, 124, 132, 207;
Rex Features 1, 129, 133a, 171, 195, 210, 212;
Sygma 72, 105, 211;
Topham Picture Point 126, 127, 133b, 147, 183, 206.

The Publishers have made every effort to trace copyright holders of material reproduced in this book and
accompanying CD. If, however, they have inadvertently
made any error, they would be grateful for notification.

(Page 1) Princess Diana a few months before her tragic
death, on an anti-landmine publicity tour in Angola, see
page 208.
(Pages 2-3) BBC War Correspondent Frank Gillard
recording a VE day broadcast from the ruins of Kassel
in Germany, 1945, see page 42.
(Opposite) A British trooper stands guard over
Argentine soldiers captured at Goose Green during the
Falklands conflict in 1982, see page 148.

Contents

Foreword

I WAS ON MY WAY HOME FROM A particularly convivial dinner a few days before Christmas 1988, thankful that I was not scheduled to be presenting *Today* the following morning and could sleep off my hangover, when the taxi driver asked me if I had heard? 'Heard what?' I asked. 'Lockerbie. They've blown up a jumbo and it's fallen on Lockerbie.'

When I opened my front door the light was flashing on my answerphone, and a few hours later I was watching the sun come up over that devastated little town and preparing to broadcast the horror of it all to an outraged nation from a converted caravan.

I suppose I could have told the boss to send another presenter – preferably someone who'd had less to drink – but it never occurred to me. We reporters define our lives by the stories we cover and we all want 'the big one' – the story that has the announcer saying: 'We interrupt this programme…'

That's why this book holds such fascination, and not just for journalists like me. We are all involved in the great news stories of our time to some extent. We are scared when the president of the most powerful nation on earth is assassinated, or shocked when a mad man fires indiscriminately in a school full of small children, or elated when our football team scores a great victory over an old enemy. We share the joy of the parents of the world's first test tube baby and the fears of our soldiers setting off to war and the celebrations when they return victorious.

But how do you pick a mere 20 stories from all those great events that have made a mark on our collective consciousness? Peter Barnard has turned to the BBC's own news coverage and has told his dramatic stories from the unique perspective of the world's oldest broadcaster, skilfully mining precious nuggets from its unrivalled archives.

He has unearthed some fascinating details that intrigue even old BBC hands like me. I try to imagine the restrictions placed on my predecessors and their bosses by the politicians of their day and compare it with the rough-and-tumble in the *Today* studio every morning.

But modern broadcasters would be foolish to patronize those pioneers whose rules were still being formulated, whose equipment was so primitive and whose resources were so limited. Some of the recordings on the disc that accompanies this book may be a little scratchy, the sound less than perfect compared with the digital purity of today, but I challenge you to listen to much of it and fail to be moved either to smiles or tears.

Good broadcasting is about more than technical proficiency or even competent journalism. It's about drama and emotion and the ability to make you feel you were there just at that moment when the announcer says: 'We interrupt this programme…'

JOHN HUMPHRYS

Introduction

WHEN THE WORLD WOKE UP ON the morning of Sunday 31 August 1997, it was to an alarm call of the most stupendous kind. The clock radio beside my bed appeared at first to have stirred itself on the wrong day, for surely the voices coming from it belonged to the *Today* team and surely Radio 4's flagship breakfast show always took Sundays off? Not on that day. *Today*'s presenters had been summoned from their beds in the middle of the night. Diana, Princess of Wales, was dead in a Paris car crash. I spent fully 20 minutes listening to the story unfold before the journalist in me stirred and I rushed to the telephone. I would write about the death that day and for many days to come.

My own brief from *The Times* was to analyse the media coverage of Diana's death and its aftermath. That duty acted as an unwitting primer for the writing of this book, for Diana's death was a perfect example of what real news is all about: the sudden occurrence of a completely unpredictable event. Even that modest definition will have its challengers. Most people in the news business have their favourite definitions but few of them really satisfy the brief. I rather like the first part of Evelyn Waugh's *Scoop*: 'News is what a chap who doesn't care much about anything wants to read'. But the rest of Waugh's caustic comment is surely more amusing than definitive: 'And it's only news until he's read it. After that it's dead.' That may be true of the routine announcements from official sources that come dressed as news every day, but it is the very opposite of the truth when applied to great events. I have found enormous fascination in reading about news stories of which I have no personal memory. And the ones I do recall have taken on a fresh excitement the more I have studied them.

Of course one has to take extreme care in judging the impact of any news story, not least because age plays a role in perception. Most people who were adults on the November day in 1963 when President John F Kennedy was assassinated have at some time been asked the question: 'Where were you when Kennedy was shot?' Remarkably, most of them know the answer, or feel the question to be sufficiently valid that they come up with a plausible response. Unfortunately time can make fools of those who assume too much about great news events, a reality demonstrated in an American cartoon that showed a middle-aged man asking his much-younger girlfriend where she had been when she heard of Kennedy's death. The girl looked at the man, aghast: 'You mean Teddy Kennedy's been shot?' By now, a Kennedy death first brings to mind the aircraft crash that killed John Kennedy Jnr in July 1999

That does not make what happened that day in Dallas in 1963 any less important, it merely makes it more in need of context. The stories in this book stand for themselves as momentous events, but they also have something to say about the time in which they happened. From the General Strike of 1926 through the English World Cup victory 40 years later, to the fall of the Berlin Wall and the numbing horror of the slaughter of little children at Dunblane in 1996, these events

In 1969 man first landed on the moon. Hundreds of millions of people around the world watched the event on television. But for those born in the 1970s the achievement has little meaning.

speak of their time and demand to be seen as part of the broader canvas. Sometimes we invest isolated incidents with more 'meaning' than they warrant, but more often the search for significance yields a dividend that helps our understanding of the world.

The thread that links all of the stories in this book is that they happened during the first 75 years of radio, a medium that was a dream when the century began. When the British Broadcasting Company, as it was first called, did get started, a man called Arthur Burrows secured himself a place in broadcasting history. On 14 November 1922, Burrows read the first regular news broadcast from the BBC, transmitted at 6 p.m. from Marconi House in the Strand. Most listeners were using headphones; a few of the better-off had installed loudspeakers. The contents of the bulletin had been supplied by the Reuters news agency because at that time the BBC had no news gathering operation of its own. There had even been scepticism about whether the BBC should get involved in news at all, but the sceptics were not to be heard very long or very loud. Four years after Burrows first read a bulletin, the General Strike silenced newspapers and turned the embryonic BBC into the nation's prime source of information.

The emphasis in this book on the way the BBC reported the news as well as the news itself is important. How we learn about events can influence our attitude to them. Telegrams have disappeared from the armoury of communication but no one who ever received one could forget the moment when their stomach turned over at the prospect of some terrible piece of news. The medium had become the message, or part of it, long before Marshall McLuhan came up with that (rather simplistic) phrase in his 1960s book, *Understanding Media*.

In the case of the BBC, the tone of the news message has a particular sensitivity. The public service remit means that objectivity is a vital necessity. Notwithstanding occasional prickly outbursts from politicians (they get grumpy at being dragged from their beds into the *Today* programme's radio car, but they

rarely refuse), most people feel that they can trust the BBC's news reports. In spite of a vast increase in the number of radio networks and television channels, I believe there is still a sense of community when great events unfold. On those occasions, our instinct is to turn to the national broadcaster.

One of the fascinations of delving into audio history has been the discovery that the notion of the early BBC as a quaint cottage industry, collecting news by carrier pigeon and disseminating it via announcers in frock coats may be colourful, but it sells the participants short. Those working for the BBC in its early days were pioneers, certainly, but they were hard-headed pioneers with enormous skill and levels of energy that drove the great broadcasting project forward at a tremendous rate. We marvel (or recoil) at the speed of technological change at the turn of the twentieth century but the first years of the BBC were marked by progress as rapid as anything that is happening in the era of digital and satellite communication. Now, we can hear and watch news unfolding. But 70 years ago, radio provided instant access to many great events, even if the engineering required filled a lorry then with the capacity that would fit in a pocket now.

Within days of the first broadcasts from Marconi House, the BBC opened transmitters in Birmingham and Manchester. The first outside broadcast came on 8 January 1923, less than three months after the BBC was founded. Late in 1923, there was an experimental broadcast to America and a first transmission, by landline, from continental Europe. In May 1924 the BBC opened its new centre at Savoy Hill just off the Strand, where the studio walls were lined with five miles of sacking to improve acoustics. November that year brought the first live outside broadcast, from the Lord Mayor's show in London. In January 1927, by which time the British Broadcasting Company had metamorphosed into the British Broadcasting Corporation, there was the first live

The Berlin Wall was taken down in 1989. Its significance as a news story was twofold. It ended 28 years of separation between the two Germanys and it marked the end of the Cold War.

commentary from a sports event, the England v Wales rugby international at Twickenham. Before that year was over there would be live commentaries on the FA Cup Final, the Grand National, the Boat Race, cricket, Wimbledon tennis and Trooping the Colour. The speed of progress was proof of a truism that still drives broadcasting technology today: once it can be done, it is only a matter of time before it can be done almost anywhere.

No technology, old or modern, is of the slightest use unless its human masters are using it wisely. News gathering is, at its best, a noble calling and reporters, although disliked as a breed by the public, carry out an essential task. They are the eyes and ears of the people. The reporters work is often pure drudgery and bears comparison with fishing from a riverbank; long periods of hanging about followed by frantic bursts of activity. BBC reporters who covered the events in this book rarely had any idea what story might emerge when they were first despatched to the scene. Whether it was landing with Allied troops at Normandy in 1944 or covering the Conservative Party conference at Brighton 40 years later, no reporter could have predicted what the story would have become when the deadline arrived.

So how have the events included in this book been chosen? Why the massacre at Dunblane, but not the one at Hungerford? Why include the shooting of John Lennon but not that of Martin Luther King? These and other questions demonstrate that to some extent

news judgements are subjective, but there is also a more reasoned explanation for the inclusions and exclusions here. Almost a century of news can only properly be sampled through a variety of ingredients. With the arrival of universal suffrage in Britain and in countless other countries, this has been, as much as anything, a century of politics and democracy. Yet only John F Kennedy and Margaret Thatcher get chapters in this book and that is because the manner of their leaving politics was so dramatic. Elections are not normally sensational events in themselves, but the shooting of Kennedy and the deposing of Thatcher had qualities that were almost theatrical. They were real news.

And some stories are here because they say something about an era. The England World Cup victory in 1966 represented more than victory in a football match, it was the high point of a decade which brought huge social change: sexual liberation via the birth pill and (in Britain) homosexual law reform, the arrival of London as something of a fashion capital after the drudgery of the post-war years and the simultaneous elevation of British popular music to a status that had seemed, until The Beatles, the permanent preserve of the United States. The birth of Louise Brown, the first test-tube baby, in 1978 is emblematic in another way: here was an event, extraordinary in itself, which opened an era of dramatic and controversial developments in medicine.

But enough scene setting. We interrupt this introduction for news that Britain has gone on strike…

The General Strike 1926

Miners' revolt sparks first complete shutdown of British industry

With public transport closed down, a woman gets a lift from a motor cyclist in central London.

IN ORDER TO UNDERSTAND FULLY the BBC's role in the General Strike that paralysed Britain for 10 days in 1926, it would be useful to begin on Epsom Downs a few weeks earlier in the same year. The 1926 running of the Derby may not seem to have much to do with a strike but the BBC's coverage of the race on radio does a lot to explain the extreme delicacy and circumspection that was to attend its coverage of the dispute. John Reith, general manager of the BBC since its creation in 1922, had fought a valiant but uphill battle against the government for more flexibility as to what the BBC could and could not cover. One concession he gained was that the BBC would be able to cover certain sporting events.

However, such were the restrictions imposed that when a BBC crew decamped to Epsom for the 1926 Derby, the first time the BBC had covered the race, they were under strict instructions. Only the sound of the race could be transmitted, which meant the noise of the crowd and the clop of the horses' hooves over the turf. The result? No, the result could not be broadcast. In the event, the coverage was absurd. It rained all day and the ground was so soft that the horses' hooves made no sound that was discernible to a microphone. Most of the crowd was huddled under umbrellas well away from the side of the course, so little was heard of them, either. It was an eerie and essentially pointless broadcast, although the BBC had made one important point just by being present. The reason for this extraordinary state of affairs

was in turn to have a vital effect on the relationship between broadcasting and the newspaper industry, which, until the coming of radio, had been the dominant conduit for news in Britain. If the reporting of a horse race could be ringfenced with restrictions, what might happen when the BBC tried to report a pitched battle between the nation's workforce and its government? The nation, and the BBC, were soon to find out.

The 7 p.m. restriction was only one of the impediments. Another was that the BBC could only broadcast news coming from existing news agencies, mostly Reuters. This meant that, whereas the newspapers had their own reporters, the BBC was restricted to news that was universally available to everyone. It was hardly a level playing field. In addition, for the duration of the General Strike, the government had imposed on the BBC a man with a fancy title who was effectively a censor. And this man, JCC Davidson, the Deputy Chief Civil Commissioner, officially known as the 'link' between the BBC and the cabinet during the strike, was to prove a key influence on the way the BBC reported the most momentous news event in the short history of the new national broadcaster.

Whole books have been written arguing about the true origins of the General Strike, some of their authors citing trade union legislation going back to 1906, others highlighting the dissatisfaction felt by workers returning to the 'land fit for heroes' after World

was fear: the government's fear of giving the BBC too much power too soon. Added to that there had been intense lobbying of the government from the newspaper industry. Already, the BBC was banned from putting out a news bulletin before 7 p.m. because it was felt that daytime bulletins would hit the sales of provincial evening newspapers. In spite of this rather half-baked service, by December 1925 Reith was able to tell a House of Lords inquiry that radio was already a boom medium, with an audience that had reached more than 10 million in three years. During the same cross-examination Reith called for Parliament to end the 7 p.m. watershed for news. This and other appeals from the embryonic BBC were to have a vital influence on the conduct and reporting of the General Strike in 1926, and the strike

War I ended in 1918. Reduced to its essentials, the strike began as a walkout by coalminers over a new pay and conditions package, which reduced their wages and increased their hours. The miners' strikes of 1974 and 1984 demonstrated that this was a sector that still had considerable, albeit dwindling power, but in the 1920s miners were top of the heap in terms of industrial muscle. The Miners Federation of Great Britain comprised a score of trade unions, some of them split into county associations, which were themselves federations of smaller unions. Coal was the fuel that drove Britain; the country's power stations were fuelled by it and virtually every home in the country had a coal fire. The biggest coalfields were in South Wales, with 149,000 miners, Yorkshire had 140,000, Durham 120,000 and Scotland 80,000. The national federation had some 722,000 members all told. A strike involving all of them constituted a national crisis, even without the support of other unions. However, that support was quickly in place. The Trades Union Congress got behind the miners and other unions went on strike. Until the settlement on 12 May, the whole country was in the grip of the strike. True, many industries carried on normally. True, even some members of the striking unions went to work. But the overall impact was so serious that, as the strike began, an edict from Buckingham Palace decreed that Britain was in a state of emergency.

The strike was declared on Saturday 1 May. It actually started when work shifts ended on the evening of the following Monday. A TUC instruction calling the strike went to the miners, transport trades, printers, power workers, iron and steel trades, builders, health workers and many more.

By 5 May, even London taxi drivers had stopped work. There were eleventh-hour debates in Parliament and a series of meetings and letters between the union leaders and Stanley Baldwin, the Prime Minister, who had personally involved himself in the negotiations with the miners' leaders. None of these appeals had any effect. The King had signed the proclamation declaring a state of emergency on the night of 30 April for issue the next day. Various Orders in Council were also signed, giving local authorities special powers. The miners' slogan, 'not a penny off the pay, not a minute on the day', was to be heard up and down the land.

With the newspapers mostly silenced by the strike, the government had no choice but to allow the BBC more bulletins. A TUC General Council statement, reported in the *Daily Herald* of 3 May, noted that the government had 'commandeered the British Broadcasting Company'. This was overstating the case, though not by all that much. Reith had long argued that the BBC should 'play its full part in national life' and it looked as if he was to get the chance at last. But the sudden pre-eminence of the BBC as a communicator during a crisis was to prove a double-edged sword, even though Reith would write later in terms that suggested he fully supported the BBC role as an arm of government. He said in an internal memo to BBC staff when the strike was over: 'Since the BBC was a national institution, and since the government in this crisis (was) acting for the people, the BBC was for the government in this crisis, too'.

One forceful illustration of the difficulties confronting the BBC during the strike came

THE LEV

when the Archbishop of Canterbury, having consulted fellow churchmen from other denominations, produced a manifesto aimed at settling the dispute. The Archbishop wanted to broadcast this manifesto, which called on both sides to make concessions and return to the negotiating table, but Davidson forbade Reith from allowing it to go ahead. Instead, the Archbishop's words appeared in a left-wing newspaper, the *British Worker*. But another Archbishop did get his words on to the BBC during the strike. This was Cardinal Francis Bourne, the Roman Catholic Archbishop of Westminster. What he had to say was clearly

CONSTITUTIONAL GOVERNMENT

...EAKS.

Contemporary cartoonist Bernard Partridge's comment on the conflict between the unions and the government.

Westminster Cathedral today…' Radio 5 Live, eat your heart out.

Cardinal Bourne made it clear during that High Mass what Catholics ought to be thinking about the strike: 'The time through which we are now passing is of exceptional character and the present strike is of a nature quite unlike any others that have preceded it. It is necessary that the Catholics should have clearly before their minds the moral principles that are involved. First, there is no moral justification for a General Strike of this character. It is a direct challenge to a lawfully constituted authority and inflicts, without adequate reason, immense discomfort and injury upon millions of our fellow countrymen. It is therefore a sin against the obedience which we owe to God…'

That kind of statement was to influence the way many people perceived BBC coverage of the strike. Part of the problem was that long statements such the Cardinal's, read by a BBC announcer, came across as if BBC opinion was being expressed. In that particular case, Reith undoubtedly shared Bourne's view. But in general, the construction of bulletins in those days tended to give the impression of a hectoring approach that upset some listeners. Overall, the small team of BBC journalists who compiled the daily bulletins, working from a room in the Admiralty, kept a balance between the two sides. But there were still plenty of people, then as now, who saw 'balance' as 'bias'. One of their complaints concerned not so much what the

more acceptable to the government position. The BBC bulletin in which an announcer read the Cardinal's words serves, incidentally, as a reminder that these were gentler times, when news was conveyed at a pace that would frustrate the busy modern listener. Bulletins even had introductions and sub-headings, in the manner of newspapers of the time. So the bulletin carrying Cardinal Bourne's words began: 'Here is the last news bulletin for today. General Situation section. The following items of news indicate the general situation in the country. Copyright in these items is reserved outside the British Isles. At the High Mass in

BBC said as what it did not say. The miners, from any standpoint, undoubtedly had a case. An agreement to improve their wages and conditions, signed only a couple of years before the strike, was effectively being torn up and put into reverse. The BBC's modern reporting is marked by this kind of contextual analysis, but it was not so in the 1920s.

Though the strike was peaceful for the most part, there was rioting in parts of the country, arrests and imprisonment. These were reported, but as exceptional events and in a low-key manner. There was a tone to the BBC coverage of cheerful stoicism, as if the country was at war with an alien force (a notion which many in government, muttering darkly about communist influences in the unions, undoubtedly supported). The Labour MP for Middlesbrough, Ellen Wilkinson, said in a letter

to *Radio Times* shortly after the strike: 'The attitude of the BBC during the strike caused pain and indignation to many subscribers. I travelled by car over 2000 miles during the strike and addressed very many meetings. Everywhere the complaints were bitter that a national service subscribed to by every class should have given only one side of the dispute. Personally I feel like asking the Postmaster General for my licence fee back.'

Ellen Wilkinson was neither the first nor the last person to write to *Radio Times* in those terms and letters about perceived BBC bias have littered the magazine's columns for all its history. Indeed, the BBC was hardly on the air before it was being accused of a Tory bias one day and a Labour bias the next. A high proportion of the complaints came to the BBC with Surrey postmarks, that leafy county in the

(Left) Striking engineers march across Blackfriars Bridge, London, in protest against the 'lock out' by employers.
(Below) Soldiers were called in to guard installations such as this bus garage, where all the drivers went on strike.

London commuter belt apparently having a large number of people who thought that BBC news bulletins contained what one letter called 'communist propaganda'. These complaints seemed especially odd given that all the BBC's bulletins were drawn from the Reuters news agency, which has never been noted as a den of communists. This steady trickle of complaints could not have come as a surprise to Reith, who had received a warning as early as 1923 about the sensitivity attached to industrial reporting. In March of that year the BBC broadcast a talk about a strike by builders in London while the strike was still going on. The strike was of little consequence nationally and the talk contained nothing that would be regarded as contentious now, but an MP complained about it in the House of Commons. The government responded by saying that it was wrong for broadcasting to be used for 'speculative matters' and a letter was sent to the BBC in

those terms. Given that the BBC was directly answerable to the Postmaster General, who had been charged with the dangerously vague duty to ensure that programmes were broadcast 'to the reasonable satisfaction of the Postmaster General', it was a warning Reith had to take seriously.

So BBC bulletins on the General Strike tended towards the upbeat. On Wednesday 9 May, the 10 a.m. bulletin started: 'Home Office reports from all parts of the country this morning indicate that the position yesterday was quieter than on any previous day of the strike. The government's energetic protective measures, prompt and severe police court action and the restraining influence of responsible trade union leaders have effectively

suppressed tendencies to rowdyism. There have been more defections from the ranks of the strikers but the position as a whole is still one of deadlock.'

The tendency to rowdyism had not been entirely suppressed even at that late stage of the dispute. More than 80 miners were arrested outside Doncaster, Yorkshire, after a clash with the police and in Poplar, London, 12 people were injured when police dispersed a crowd of strike sympathizers. But that was the dispute's last hurrah: at noon, the General Council of the TUC arrived at 10 Downing Street to tell Baldwin that the strike was over.

The news was broadcast on the BBC at 1 p.m., in spite of last-ditch attempts by the Communist Party of Great Britain to get the workers to stay on strike. Baldwin made a statement to the Commons that afternoon, including in it the first parliamentary use of that

now timeworn phrase 'a victory of common sense'. King George V issued a statement, headed 'To My People', calling for everyone involved to bring into being 'a peace which will be lasting, because, forgetting the past, it looks only to the future with the hopefulness of a united people'.

That and other manifestations of optimism were to prove premature, for the strike was to rumble on for some days, with some unions refusing to return to work. Some employers, notably the railways, decreed that all the strikers were deemed to have dismissed themselves and would in future only be employed if they signed individual contracts. Nonetheless, our old friend Cardinal Bourne ordered that a *Te Deum* be sung in Westminster Cathedral. The BBC entered into a positive orgy of celebration, carrying the King's message shortly after 7 p.m. and a message from the Prime Minister at 9.30 p.m. That was followed by a quite extraordinary moment in the history of British broadcasting, when Reith decided to broadcast a valedictory message. The text of that message acts a primer for those wishing to understand Reith, a deeply religious, moral man who loved his country, a man who was the work ethic made manifest. Reith, speaking in his familiar stentorian tones, told the nation: 'Our first feelings on hearing of the termination of the General Strike must be of profound thankfulness to Almighty God who has led us through this supreme test with national health unimpaired. You have heard the message from the King and the Prime Minister. It remains only to add the conviction that the nation's happy escape has been in large measure due to the personal trust in the Prime Minister (which was) not misplaced. As for the BBC, we hope your confidence in, and goodwill to, us have not suffered. We have laboured under certain difficulties, the full story of which may be told some day. We have tried to help. In going back to work tomorrow, or the next day, can we not all go as fellow-craftsmen, resolved in the determination to pick the up broken pieces, repair the gaps, and build the walls of a more enduring city – the city revealed to the mystical eyes of William Blake when he wrote…' At which point Reith rounded off his broadcast by reading out all four verses of Blake's *Jerusalem*.

On the morning after the night before, the BBC's 10 a.m. bulletin brought the nation down out of the Reithian clouds: 'As far as London was concerned, the calling off of the General Strike seemed to make little difference to traffic this morning. Few of the strikers have returned to work and the strike service of trains and buses is still in force… No trams were running in the early morning and the scramble to get to work was as bad as ever…' Over the next few days the strike slowly petered out, with the employers and the unions slightly amending their positions. The miners went back to work after gaining agreement that their pre-strike terms and conditions would remain in force. The railway workers were reinstated when the employers agreed to take them back on their previous contracts and the unions in turn admitted acting 'wrongfully' in calling the strike.

This is not the place to assess the winners and losers: arguments on those matters have raged in trade union circles from the day the strike ended to this. But the strike did have one clear winner, and that was the BBC. Its coverage may have angered some people and there is no question that Reith steered a course that was very much on the government side of the river. But Reith had the longer term to think about. The timing of the General Strike could not have been worse from the BBC's standpoint. In 1925, a few months before the strike began, the BBC's licence had been extended for only two years. In effect the BBC spent the strike on probation. When it ended, Reith appeared to have passed the test. Early in 1927 the British Broadcasting Company became the British Broadcasting Corporation, with much more freedom to operate, more news bulletins, more sporting events, and with Reith as its first Director-General.

The Wall Street Crash 1929

Stock market crash causes ruin, leading to America's Great Depression

Desperate measures were taken as investors struggled to pay off debts when the stock market crashed.

TOWARDS THE END OF MARCH 1999
there was a day of great of celebration along Wall Street, heart of the New York financial district. Bells rang out in the stock exchange, dealers yelped and yelled and clapped their hands, and champagne corks fizzed through the air like missiles. The reason for the fun and games was not some mammoth deal. It was merely that the Dow Jones Industrial Average, the key index of Wall Street stock trading, had passed the 10,000 mark. It was soon to fall back, but there are psychological levels in stock markets that carry at least as much importance for those who work in them as any interest rate cut or balance of payments surplus. All markets are inherently bullish and dealers in them operate in an environment that is largely insulated from the real world outside. The push past 10,000 did not say anything, either way, about the general state of the American economy. But there were a few nervous voices raised, some who looked over their shoulders to a date in history that had shaken not just Wall Street, but the whole world.

Seventy years before the 1999 red-letter day, on 24 October 1929, the New York police riot squads had been summoned to Wall Street to control a vast crowd of people who had gathered at the scene of what appeared to be a disaster. The crowd was hysterical, shouting, stamping, calling for news. At the headquarters of the JP Morgan Bank, executives from all the leading banks had gathered to discuss the collapse of the stock market. That morning, there had been an unprecedented wave of selling, with nearly 13 million shares changing

hands: a fantastic amount for those days. Stock
in the huge and successful Radio Corporation
(RCA), one of the bellwethers of American
industry at the time, was trading at 45, having
been at 114 earlier in the year. Countless other
blue chip companies had millions wiped off
their share values. Individual investors, many of
whom had borrowed to buy shares, found
themselves ruined. Since the crash, many myths
and legends have grown about what happened
that day, including reports of mass suicides as
bankers jumped from Wall Street windows.
These reports were exaggerated, but there
were undoubtedly some suicides: in one case,
two men who held a joint share trading

account jumped to their deaths, hand in hand,
from a window ledge at the Ritz hotel.

When the meeting at the Morgan bank
ended, Thomas W Lamont, a senior partner in
the bank, stepped into the street to utter one
of the great understatements of the century:
'There has been a little distress selling on the
Stock Exchange,' he said. The situation was
'technical rather than fundamental'. Lamont
reckoned that the market was undergoing a
period of 'readjustment' after four years of
relentless buying. In a sense Lamont was
right, but his words hardly did justice to the
extraordinary events that preceded the
crash and the equally extraordinary events that

The scene on Black Thursday when thousands of workers and investors gathered at the start of what was to prove the Great Depression.

were to follow it, with effects well beyond America's shores. The Wall Street crash had consequences, direct and indirect, in Europe and the rest of the world, although the Depression that hit America in the 1930s had already occurred, a decade earlier, in Britain. The Wall Street crash was to dominate BBC radio news broadcasts in late 1929. The BBC had carried out an experimental broadcast to America in November 1923 and the first transatlantic relay was laid in November 1924. The new landline across the Atlantic meant that the BBC was able to carry reports from the US and that facility was to become important in covering the fast-moving story from New York in 1929.

This was not to be one of those heart-stopping news stories to which aghast listeners woke up one morning. No cherished public figure died, no much-loved institution had been blown to smithereens. The Wall Street crash was just as sensational in its way as any assassination or natural disaster, but as a news story it had the qualities of a marathon rather than a sprint. One reason for this was its complexity. Even now, historians are not entirely agreed as to which particular day was

the crash's defining moment (24 October was only one candidate). And this was, on the face of it, a financial story full of jargon to do with margin calls and technical corrections that appeared to involve only people rich enough to trade in the stock market. In Britain that impression was certainly prevalent, for it was not until the Thatcher era of the 1980s that share ownership as an activity for the common man or woman was to become, if not commonplace, then widespread. Share ownership was a much more egalitarian activity in the United States, even in the 1920s (about two million American investors were directly affected by the crash). Indeed some of the seeds of the cataclysmic events of 1929 were to be found in get-rich-quick schemes that ordinary Americans had been encouraged to join. They could even own shares without paying for them, another of the factors which was to bring down the market on their heads. So the crash had some of the characteristics of its motorway equivalent: a coming together of disparate elements, seemingly in slow motion, with everyone blaming everyone else after the event. But the fact that the Wall Street crash was a multiple pile-up with many casualties and consequences a long way down the road is not in doubt.

The origins of the crash can be traced to a much earlier date and they are social as much as financial. The US entered World War I only in 1917, the year before it ended, but American servicemen returning from the European war still brought a new moral outlook that had been picked up, mostly, in the bordellos of

France. The full implementation of this new ethos was slightly delayed by the slump of 1920-22 but in every area of life thereafter a different, more restless and energetic approach to life became apparent. From 1922 onwards America was on a roll of production, prosperity and social upheaval, that last going ahead despite Prohibition, which was the last hurrah of the founding Puritans, the finger in the dyke of inevitable change. The drive for prosperity came from a combination of individual entrepreneurs and technological change, the latter manifesting itself in the tremendous growth of the car industry: Americans owned 6.7 million cars in 1919, and nearly 23 million in 1929. Spending on clothing rose enormously as fashion became, well, fashionable. Religious leaders spoke out against the 'decadence' of the Charleston and were no less censorious about the dresses being worn by its dancers. The wearing of skirts that were ten inches above the ankle was described as 'excessive nudity'. In Britain, a Dr J S Russell told the Institute of Hygiene that young women were turning to drink and drugs to fuel their hectic lifestyles: 'Scarcely has the age of 20 been reached before the lines that belong to the face of a woman of middle age have become evident in such girls'. Other medical men railed against young women who did not eat enough, apparently in pursuit of the 'willowy figures' they saw on fashion catwalks. Anorexic models are by no means an invention of the late twentieth century. These factors gave what was going on in Britain and America a notional link, but there was a key difference. In Britain this

new abandon was being exercised in a country still going through a slump, whereas in America the behavioural change was in large measure a product of the new prosperity. Few people thought it could ever end.

As late as January 1928, the new American President, Calvin Coolidge, would say in his State of the Union address that America had never in its history surveyed 'a more pleasing prospect ... tranquillity and contentment ... years of prosperity'.

Nor did Coolidge have any doubt as to where the credit lay: 'The main source of these unexampled blessings lies in the integrity and character of the American people'. Coolidge appears to have been either unaware of or unconcerned by the fact that, in terms of the rise of the stock market, much of this apparent

wreckage of the crash, they would see that the increase in share trading throughout the decade had been phenomenal. The number of shares traded on the New York Stock Exchange in 1920 was 227 million, by 1929 it had risen to 1.125 billion. But there were peaks and troughs along the way, notably in the middle of the decade when a land boom in Florida fuelled an orgy of investment only for the boom, and the market, to collapse. That might have acted as a warning, but it did not. Between 1926 and 1928 share prices roared ahead and they continued on up, largely because of a technical sounding device called 'margin'. This was to prove the agent of the market's destruction. Margin was the way that the ordinary person could get himself a slice of the stock market, because it meant that one could buy, say, $1,000 worth of stocks by putting down only $100. The stockbroker effectively borrowed the rest of the money on behalf of the investor. If this sounds like a dodgy way to proceed now, there were plenty of supposedly knowledge-able people willing to encourage it then.

Several banks led the way in selling the investment scheme to ordinary Americans, men and women. The scheme worked because a climate had been created in which Americans had become convinced that they had a right, bordering on a duty, to make a lot of money. Only a few months before the crash, *Ladies*

prosperity was founded on money borrowed to buy shares. This money was touted to ordinary Americans by hard-nosed salesmen who might as well have been selling snake-oil remedies. In his seminal book, *The Great Crash of 1929*, the economist JK Galbraith noted: 'One thing should have been visible even to Coolidge. It concerned the American people of whom he had spoken so well. Along with the sterling qualities he praised, they were also displaying an inordinate desire to get rich quickly with the minimum of effort.' Thus did Galbraith contribute the phrase 'get rich quick' to the lexicon of modern economic life.

The rise of the New York stock market through the 1920s was neither inexorable nor consistent. When analysts looked back from the

Home Journal ran an article by a leading Democrat politician and the director of General Motors. The headline said it all: 'Everybody ought to be rich'. Loans to buy shares grew at an astonishing rate between 1926 and 1929, when they reached more than six billion dollars. Galbraith and other economists knew that borrowing at this level to fund stock purchases in a market that was intrinsically voluble had the potential for disaster, but who listens to economists? In any event, the margin system appeared to be working well enough. All it needed was a rising market, because the increase in the value of the stocks paid for the debt incurred in buying them. If, that is, they kept on rising.

In June of 1929 after a few months of the usual yo-yoing, the New York stock market began another upward surge. Blue chip stocks like General Electric rose 50 per cent or more in three months. That was a sign of the keenness to invest in new technologies that is demonstrated now by the scramble to buy into Internet stocks. Nothing much happened in the early autumn and the few observers who were worried about the state of the market, notably the Editor of the *New York Times*, were not being listened to. Most people mistook the late summer calm for stability, forgetting perhaps that there is nothing as quiet as an ambush. There was a sharp downward movement in September, but that soon passed. There were also, and more worryingly, signs of industrial decline, with even car manufacturing dropping from its previous high levels. That and other indicators have led some to say that the Wall Street crash was triggered by economic recession. But a greater number of economists argue that even if a recession was coming it had not yet started and there was no reason to think that, even if the economic downturn worsened, the Federal Reserve – America's central bank – would not ease interest rates to cope with the situation.

On Sunday 19 October 1929, the *New York Times* carried this headline: 'Stocks driven down as wave of selling engulfs market'. There had been a six-point fall in the Dow Jones on the

Friday and more selling on Saturday. The headlines must have contributed to a further fall on the Monday, but there was as yet no reason to think that something spectacular was about to happen.

Financial crashes tend to attract labels that involve the word 'black': the one in Britain in October 1987 (October seems to be a wicked month for stock markets) is the most recent British example. So a measure of the scale of the disaster that hit Wall Street in 1929 is the fact that it had not one but two black days: Black Thursday, 24 October, and Black Tuesday, 29 October. The latter was actually worse than the former, but Black Thursday continues to be the universal epithet applied to the Wall Street crash (though in terms of what actually happened in the market, Black Monday in 1987 was worse than either of them). The Wall Street crash is more significant for what followed. Black Thursday brought an unprecedented level of trading on Wall Street: almost 13 million shares changed hands. Matters were made worse by the fact that the ticker tape system through which share prices were communicated to others had never been able to keep up with a heavy volume of trading, so there were long gaps between updates. Traders knew what was happening because they were there, but few people outside the building, and even fewer outside New York, had more than an inkling of what was going on.

Shortly after lunch, the rumour mill went into overdrive when word spread that the big banks were about to launch a support operation, which basically involved buying up huge numbers of shares. This rumour proved to be correct and was to produce a moment that Wall Street traders still talk about at dinner parties. Richard Witney, a broker with the Morgan bank, walked on to the floor of the exchange and issued the following bid: '205 for 10,000 steel'. That purchase, and others that Witney made the same afternoon, halted the fall. But it was a stay of execution rather than a reprieve. The market was in freefall. Untold numbers of investors were going bankrupt every hour. There was no cash to meet margin calls, the moment when the balance of the money used to buy stocks had to be found. The theory, that the balance would come from the profits on the shares, fell apart when the market collapsed. After a few days in which the market moved very little (but always downward), there followed Black Tuesday, 29 October. The day before, the Dow had opened at 298, more than a fifth below its peak, but by the end of the Tuesday it was at 230. More than 16 million shares were traded that day. The collapse continued and the Dow reached its lowest point of the year, 198, in the middle of November.

After the fall, came the fall. The American economy collapsed, in spite of a false dawn on the stock market in spring 1930 when the Dow briefly rallied. The problem was a collapse of confidence. Car production, so buoyant through most of the 1920s, fell by almost 75 per cent in the last few months of 1930. Commodity prices fell. There were successive stock market rallies, each raising hopes that were brutally dashed. Banks failed by the hundred. Unemployment reached nearly 14 million. This was not some calamity confined to lush business houses and stock market gamblers. The Depression that followed the Wall Street crash hit everyone. Farmers suffered terribly. In *Hard Times*, a chronicle of the Depression written by Studs Terkel, there is a quote from a farmer in Iowa: 'First they'd take your farm, then they took your livestock, then your farm machinery, even your household goods. Grain was being burned – it was cheaper than coal. In South Dakota, the county (grain) elevator listed corn at minus three cents a bushel. If you wanted to sell 'em a bushel of corn you had to bring in three cents.'

The contagion crossed the Atlantic, like an autumn fog. Stock markets in Britain, France, Germany, Italy and the Netherlands fell, London by almost 50 per cent. The situation in Germany was to become especially relevant, for in that country's economic collapse lay the seeds of the rise of Hitler. Share prices in Germany had peaked in 1927, well ahead of Wall Street. Their collapse, however, was very much on the coat tails of the Wall Street crash. In 1931, the German banking system was closed. The Germans, unlike most others, had pursued a rigorously deflationary policy which, together with the collapse of the total value of world trade (from $35 billion in 1929 to $12 billion in 1933) was to lead to massive unemployment and the subsequent exploitation by Hitler and the Nazi Party. The causes of the Depression were relatively complex, therefore the causes of the European decline were just as complex: it was so much easier to cut to the chase and blame the Jews.

So what were the causes of the 1929 crash? In a paragraph in Robert Beckman's book *Crashes: Why They Happen, What To Do*, he writes: 'The cause… is no mystery. The culmination of speculative excesses combined with excesses in production, founded on the kind of manic build-up in debt that has preceded every mega-slump in history, simply represents the seeds of its own self-destruction.' That certainly sounds right, for by October 1929 Americans were living in the foothills of a debt mountain: billions borrowed to buy shares, billions owed by farmers. But there were also factors related to America's success, especially its success as the inventor of mass production. The car industry, led by Henry Ford, was so good at making and selling cars that by 1929 more cars were being built than the makers could hope to sell. During that decade car production accounted for a staggering 10 per cent of America's gross national product.

The inevitable result of the saturation of a market on which the country was so dependent was a collapse in sales, huge job losses and a serious knock-on effect: for every factory assembling cars, there were 10 that made and supplied parts. The effect of a slump in car sales was bound to have the most severe repercussions, even without the Wall Street crash. But of course the one helped feed the other and in October of 1929, the feeding frenzy began to consume the American economy, with effects in Britain and Europe that were to be felt for many years to come.

The Abdication of Edward VIII 1936

Britain divided as Edward VIII abdicates for 'the woman I love'

The crisis polarized opinion in Britain with many people, like this protester, believing Edward should be allowed to marry and stay on the throne.

A CARTOON FROM THE 1930s SHOWS a family, father, mother and four children, standing in the middle of their living room listening to the radio. The mother is looking plaintively at her husband saying: 'Albert, I'm sure the dear King wouldn't wish us to stand to attention all the time'. The etiquette of listening to royal broadcasts in their early days was no laughing matter. At the time, when ordinary citizens were interviewed about these weighty issues, they often wondered whether they should stand whenever the National Anthem was broadcast, and whether it was all right to eat while listening to the monarch on the radio. In late 1936 there was to a be a royal broadcast that would send listeners gasping to their feet, whatever their sense of etiquette. In spite of royal divorces and other scandals late in the twentieth century, there is general agreement that the abdication of Edward VIII in 1936 was then, and remains, one of the most sensational moments in the history of broadcasting.

The creation, early in 1927, of the British Broadcasting Corporation from the old British Broadcasting Company was to give the nation's broadcasters a new impetus and pave the way for the momentous broadcast in 1936. Four years earlier, having gained a vast amount of outside broadcast experience covering sports events over the previous six years, both the BBC and Buckingham Palace felt confident enough to start broadcasting a message from the monarch at Christmas. King George V entered fully into the spirit of the thing and reading the text of his message now one can hear a monarch who was so clearly in touch with his people. Undoubtedly the 1932 and 1933 broadcasts had an extremely formal nuance, but by 1934 the King was gaining in confidence. He was advised to be more relaxed, both in manner and content. He set aside the earlier tendency to speak grandly about Britain and the Empire and instead he went for the personal touch: 'I wish you all, my dear friends, a happy Christmas. I have been deeply touched by the greetings that have reached me from all parts of the Empire. Let me in response send to each of you a greeting from myself.' King George had celebrated

his silver jubilee that year, and said in the broadcast: 'The year has been to me most memorable. It called forth a spontaneous offering of loyalty, and may I say love, which the Queen and I can never forget.'

The first Christmas broadcast, in 1932, had been so successful that the Palace more or less gave the BBC *carte blanche* to cover other state events. These were put in the hands of Robert Wood, the BBC's engineer in charge of outside broadcasts. Wood was a brilliant and resourceful young man, as indeed he needed to be. Although the King was happy to have royal events broadcast, the etiquette of these occasions presented with Wood with great difficulties. The wedding of the Duke of Kent to Princess Marina at Westminster Abbey in

November 1934 illustrates the point. This was the first royal wedding to be covered by the BBC and was Wood's toughest challenge so far. No commentator was allowed inside the main part of the abbey. Nor was Wood. He and the commentator worked from the crypt, six feet from the Tomb of the Unknown Soldier. Wood spent weeks placing microphones all over the abbey, studying timetables and pacing out the route taken by the bride and groom, so that what the commentator was saying would coincide with what was actually happening. The technology of the time did not allow for all the microphones to be 'open', that is to say, switched on, at once, therefore Wood had to know where the action was at any given moment so that he could open the relevant

**Edward, then Duke
of Windsor, meets
Maori girls during a
tour of New Zealand
in 1920.**

microphone. The broadcast was a triumph and listeners everywhere heard the couple make their vows.

George V, a gruff man who had famously said 'I don't like abroad, I've been there', died at Sandringham House in January 1936. Few people knew when the BBC covered his funeral service at Westminster Abbey that a crisis was brewing in the background that would, by the end of the year, lead to the most momentous royal broadcast so far. When the King died, the BBC – presumably after consulting the Palace – decided not to have a commentary on the funeral. This seems like a very odd decision now, but it resulted in a broadcast of quite extraordinary impact. The sounds of the funeral, clergy, hymns, horses' hooves, a murmur from the crowds, comprised an aural portrait of an event that was both moving and informative. Edward succeeded to the throne immediately and arrangements began for his coronation.

Edward was Prince of Wales when he went to a party given by his lover, Lady Furness, in 1931 and there was introduced to Wallis Simpson. Fantastic stories have attached themselves to Mrs Simpson ever since: she has been variously identified as a lesbian, a heterosexual nymphomaniac, and a spy for the Soviet KGB. She is supposed to have had an illegitimate child by an Italian count. No convincing evidence has ever been produced for these claims and the truth is more prosaic, but no less interesting. Wallis Simpson was an American who had been born Wallis Warfield in 1896, two years after the prince. She was

part of a wealthy Baltimore élite, though not one of the wealthiest and most élite parts. She was no great beauty, nor was she an intellectual: she spent little time reading, then or later, and had no interest in the arts. But she did have a quick mind. She was witty and, most significant in the context of what was to happen, she knew how to give men the kind of attention that flattered them. She married one of the men she attracted, an American naval officer, but the union was disastrous and ended in divorce. Her second marriage, to Ernest Simpson, who was in the shipping business, began in 1928. The couple lived a comfortable life in London and Wallis acquired a reputation as an attentive hostess at parties.

Her first fateful meeting with the prince was casual and inconclusive. It meant a lot to Wallis, for to be a hostess in London who could claim to know the Prince of Wales was quite a notch in one's social belt. The second meeting took place in May 1931, and in January 1932 the Simpsons spent a weekend at Fort Belvedere, the Prince's country retreat. The prince remained involved with Thelma Furness, but that inconvenience was overcome in 1934 when Lady Furness went to live in America. Lady Furness was to write later that she asked Wallis to 'look after him while I am away'. Wallis was diligent in making sure that she responded to that request.

The relationship that was to develop from that time grew almost entirely without benefit of media interest. In the context of the late twentieth century, when every brick in the edifice of collapsing royal marriages has been taken down and put through the tabloid cement mixer, it is hard to imagine there could have been a time when the heir to the throne could conduct an intimate relationship with a married woman without the general public having the slightest idea that it was going on. Indeed, a parallel set of circumstances involving the present Prince of Wales and Camilla Parker Bowles, married for much of the time that she has known the prince, but now divorced, has been remorselessly exposed to the glare of publicity for more than a decade. American and continental European newspapers and magazines commented on the Wallis Simpson relationship, but not a word of it was breathed in the British press until the crisis was nearly at boiling point.

The trouble with Wallis, so far as the British establishment was concerned, was that she was both an American and a double divorcee. The prince had always been something of a 'ladies man', as the terminology of the time had it, but those in the upper reaches of royal and political circles soon realized that the relationship was serious, in more than one meaning of the word. The prince was at least unmarried, but in the climate of the time there could be no question of the heir to the throne marrying a divorced woman. Nor was Wallis doing very much to win friends and influence people: those who had been around the prince for many years mostly regarded her with suspicion and hostility. That included the staff at Belvedere, where Wallis more or less took over, firing cooks, butlers and others and leaving what one staff member described as

'a hell of a mess' in the kitchen, where she would appear in the middle of the night to cook bacon and eggs.

For a long time King George, the prince's father, chose to ignore the relationship, but by 1935 he appears to have encouraged others to alert the prince to the dangers of his liaison with Wallis, and had banned her from court.

The prince protested about this ban, first to the Lord Chamberlain and then directly to his father. The King only lifted the ban when the prince promised him that Wallis was not actually his mistress (Edward had sued a writer who said that she was, an action that astonished his staff at Belvedere, at least one of whom had seen the couple in bed together).

But in his definitive biography of Edward VIII, Philip Ziegler convincingly makes the case that it was not sexual attraction that made the prince so devoted to Wallis. 'It was her personality which captivated him,' Ziegler

Fort Belvedere had departed she would taunt and berate him until he was reduced to tears.'

However bizarre this relationship must have seemed, it was clearly real and unlikely to end in short order. The death of King George in January 1936 brought Edward to the throne and the brought the crisis that some in government and royal circles knew was coming much closer. The new king went about royal business as if nothing was happening that might threaten his reign, but the reality was that the future of his relationship with Wallis dominated both his thoughts and those of the government throughout that year. Frantic, vain efforts were going on to prevent Wallis getting divorced for the second time. When divorce became inevitable, arrangements were made under which Ernest Simpson would commit a ritual act of adultery and Wallis would divorce him, rather than the other way round. Still Baldwin tried to get the divorce stopped, because the reporting of it would lead to a public scandal. Baldwin went to see Edward, who refused to intervene. He would neither end the relationship nor try to stop the divorce.

writes, 'She gave him something that he had never found before and which he now realized he needed desperately. All his adult life he had been surrounded by deferential courtiers and fawning hostesses. Wallis respected neither office nor man and made it abundantly plain that this was so. No Englishwoman, however assertive, however independent, however little wedded to the cause of monarchy, could have done the same. Wallis was harsh, dominating, often abominably rude. She treated the prince at best like a child who needed keeping in order, at worst with contempt. He invited it and begged for more. When the weekend guests at

(Left) After years of silence on the royal relationships, newspapers could speak of little else once the crisis became public.
(Right) One of a series of formal portraits of the couple taken by royal photographer Cecil Beaton.

The Simpson divorce hearing was in, of all places, Ipswich on 27 October, but it had been assured of only limited exposure in the press by a meeting between the King and Lord Beaverbrook, owner of the *Daily Express*, ten days earlier. The King assured Beaverbrook that it would be quite wrong to have Wallis spread all over the newspapers just because she was a friend of the King, that he had no intention of marrying Wallis and that she was getting divorced to escape a miserable marriage. Beaverbrook, who was also chairman of the newspaper proprietors, concurred and persuaded others to do the same. Only limited reports of the divorce hearing appeared in Britain, though the American press had a field day. The BBC remained silent on the matter. Meanwhile, the Baldwin government consulted the dominions. Australia was against the King being allowed to marry Wallis; Canada preferred abdication to marriage but added the rider that abdication had to come from the King rather than being imposed on him; and South Africa regarded abdication as undesirable, but not as undesirable as marrying Wallis.

The press dam eventually broke on 3 December, led not by Fleet Street but by a report in the *Yorkshire Post*. It carried an address by the Bishop of Bradford which, albeit mildly, criticized the King: 'Some of us wish that he gave more positive signs of awareness'. This only reflected the anger of the Anglican clergy, hundreds of whom were bombarding the Archbishop of Canterbury with demands that he force the King to give up Wallis. In reporting the bishop's words, the *Post* added a reference to foreign press reports about the relationship with Wallis and said: 'They plainly have a foundation in fact'. Fleet Street weighed in, some newspapers backing the King, others supporting the government view that the King could not marry Wallis. *The Times*, whose Editor, Geoffrey Dawson, had been privy to much of Baldwin's thinking on the issue, strongly sided with the government. Some newspapers supported the idea of a morganatic marriage, which would have meant that Wallis could not be Queen nor could any children of the marriage be heirs to the throne, an idea which the King favoured. But Baldwin's cabinet had already rejected this solution. With the story out and all the compromise options exhausted, the reign of King Edward VIII was, quite clearly, almost over.

The King had planned one last throw of the dice. He wanted to put the matter in the hands of the people. He would go to the BBC and broadcast to the nation, saying that he wanted to marry Wallis but that she would not become Queen. He would then leave the

Daily Mirror

No. 10306

THE DAILY MIRROR, Friday, December 11, 1936.

Registered at the G.P.O. as a newspaper

ONE PENNY

LATE · LON · ED

EDWARD VIII'S RADIO FAREWELL TO-NIGHT

THE NEW KING ARRIVES IN HIS CAPITAL

London Cheers George VI

Edward VIII will broadcast to the Empire and the world to-night as Mr. Edward Windsor, a "private individual owing allegiance to the new King."

This will follow the signing of his abdication papers and the succession to the Throne of his brother, the Duke of York, who will be 41 on Monday.

The time has been fixed tentatively for 10 p.m. During the evening Edward VIII is expected to leave the country.

THE capital welcomed its new King — who will reign as George VI — for the first time just before midnight when he arrived back at his home at 145, Piccadilly, after dining with his brother at Fort Belvedere.

A crowd of 20,000 which had waited for hours burst into wild and prolonged cheering.

The King's arrival was so sudden that his car was caught up in the homegoing theatre traffic.

Two taxis barred his entrance into his home, and through hundreds of police struggled wildly, they could not keep the surging crowd back.

People ran shouting round the royal car waving their hands, hats and handkerchiefs in the King's face.

Tired and Pale

He sat well back in his car, looking tired and pale. Obviously he was moved by the tremendous demonstration and he smiled warmly and bowed once or twice.

After being held up for quite five minutes in the crowd the car edged its way into the courtyard.

When the King stepped from the car there was more tremendous cheering. By this time the crowd was quite out of hand and swept right up to the railings of the house.

Further police were rushed to the scene and they helped to restore order.

After the King had gone indoors the great multitude stood outside and sang the National Anthem and "For He's a Jolly Good

(Continued on back page)

Britain's new King, the Duke of York, arriving home at 145, Piccadilly, last night, after dining at Fort Belvedere with his brother. Huge crowds gave the new Monarch a great welcome to his capital. (See back page).

Picture pages are 8, 12 14, 16, 17, 19 and 28.

(Left) The end of the crisis, as trailed by the *Daily Mirror*. (Right) King Edward's abdication broadcast drew a vast radio audience. In fact, there were more people wanting to hear Edward's broadcast than there were radio sets.

country while the people of Britain thought things over. After a suitable interval, he would either return with Wallis as his consort or he would remain abroad and abdicate. The scheme reached an advanced stage; rooms were reserved at a hotel in Zurich and a letter of credit was provided by Coutts Bank. Two private aircraft were waiting at Hendon airfield. When Baldwin heard about the plan, he told the King he was opposed to it personally but would consult the cabinet. His ministers supported him. There was a panicky few hours when someone said that the King might appeal directly to John Reith, the BBC's Director-General, and broadcast without government permission, but that did not happen. In any event, it was inconceivable that Reith would have agreed to the plan.

As abdication moved from likely to inevitable, countless details had to be worked out to do with titles and money and where the couple would live. Edward signed the Instrument of Abdication at Fort Belvedere on 10 December, declaring his 'irrevocable determination to renounce the throne for Myself and for My descendants'. Baldwin would announce the abdication in the Commons the following afternoon and the King, at his own insistence, would broadcast to the nation in the evening. His mother, Queen Mary, tried to talk him out of it: 'Surely you might spare yourself that extra strain and emotion?' The King was determined to speak to the people, however, a determination that was to leave for posterity one of the most remarkable broadcasts in the history of the medium. But it had still not been decided what the now former King would be called, a matter of vital importance to Reith, who would have to introduce the broadcast. Reith himself suggested 'Mr Edward Windsor'. Edward said that as the son of a duke, he could hardly be a mister. So Edward was created Duke of Windsor by his brother, now unexpectedly elevated to be King George VI, and Reith would introduce him as 'His Royal Highness, Prince Edward'.

The broadcast was relayed from Windsor Castle. Reith recalled later, in a conversation with Lord Monckton, that when he arrived at Windsor he engaged Edward in conversation about various matters, on the basis that it was

best to behave 'as if nothing untoward or specially unusual was happening'. This conjures up a wondrous vision: of two men, the one an abdicated monarch about to be exiled for the love of a woman, the other a Scottish Presbyterian about to preside over the broadcast of his life, chatting inconsequentially as if waiting for a football match to start. When the moment came for Edward to speak to the nation, he did so in terms that no one who heard it was ever likely to forget. Even now, 60 years on and in an era so markedly different in every way, the sound of Edward's voice, strained but even, is extremely moving. The key sentence in his statement, the one that has stayed in the memory of all who heard it, was: 'You must believe me when I tell you that I have found it impossible to carry the heavy burden of responsibility and to discharge my duty as King as I would wish to do, without the help and support of the woman I love'.

Most of the speech was written by Edward, though Lord Monckton had made suggestions

and there were parts of it that called to mind, correctly, the flourishes of Winston Churchill; he did indeed play a part. The ending certainly had a Churchillian ring: 'I now quit altogether public affairs, and I lay down my burden. It may be some time before I return to my native land, but I shall always follow the fortunes of the British race and Empire with profoundest interest, and if at any time in the future I can be found of service to His Majesty in a private station I shall not fail. And now we all have a new king. I wish him, and you, his people, happiness and prosperity with all my heart. God bless you all. God save the King.'

With that Edward rose from the microphone and slapped Lord Monckton on the shoulder: 'Walter, it is a far better thing I go to'. In the early hours of 12 December, the Royal Navy destroyer HMS *Fury* cast off its mooring lines and slipped out of Portsmouth harbour, carrying the Duke of Windsor to France and exile. Six months later Wallis Simpson became the Duchess of Windsor.

Britain at war with Germany as Chamberlain's appeasement policy fails

London's burning: the dome of St Paul's, proud and defiant, glows in the fires that burned all over the city.

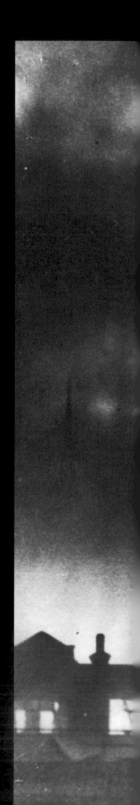

BRUCE BELFRAGE WAS READING THE 9 p.m. news at a microphone in the basement of Broadcasting House on the night of 15 October 1940. 'Tonight's talk, after this bulletin,' Belfrage said, 'will be by Lord Lloyd, the Colonial Secretary…' A tremendous crashing followed these words, conveyed through the airwaves with a realism so startling it was as if a thunderstorm had broken out inside the head of the listener. But there was a barely perceptible pause before Belfrage, in a classic example of British stiff upper lip, continued: 'The story of recent naval successes in the Mediterranean is told…' A German bomb had scored a direct hit on Broadcasting House. It plunged through the roof but did not immediately explode. The bomb ended up on the fifth floor, three floors below the roof and six above Belfrage's head, lodged behind a door.

While BBC staff and others were searching for the bomb, it exploded. Seven people were killed. The damage was immense. The BBC's gramophone library, a storehouse of priceless treasures, was wrecked. The news library suffered equally. The morning after the bombing, the librarian who ran the news library was to be found at 6 a.m., picking about in the rubble of Portland Place, hoping to salvage something of his archive. In *BBC at War*, a pamphlet written before the war ended (and sold for a pre-decimal price of sixpence), Antonia White recalled that the distressed librarian was approached and closely questioned by a police officer, who found him in the rubble and suspected him of being a looter. He was lucky not to be arrested.

Churchill's wartime broadcasts probably did more to galvanize the nation and maintain its spirit than any other single factor. Churchill had been Chancellor of the Exchequer during the 1926 General Strike and thoroughly disliked the BBC's determination to maintain at least a notional independence. Mistrust of the BBC and a failure to understand the vital role it could play in wartime meant that the Corporation's war got off to an very bad start.

Germany had invaded Poland on Friday 1 September 1939, thus making World War II inevitable. The previous year Chamberlain had held talks with Adolf Hitler in Munich, returning to wave the infamous piece of white paper and make the statement 'peace in our time' that would blight his reputation forever. The Prime Minister was already ill when he went to see Hitler, who assured him that Poland was not part of the Nazis' expansion plans. Chamberlain may or may not have believed him; few others did. Britain had a treaty obligation to Poland. Hitler clearly did not believe that Britain would go to war to honour that obligation, the first of many errors of judgement made by the Chancellor of Germany.

The bomb was one of several that brought the BBC into World War II in the most direct and violent of ways. Belfrage and his colleagues at the Corporation might not have been broadcasting at all. Neither Neville Chamberlain, Prime Minister when war was declared, nor Winston Churchill, who went to 10 Downing Street when Chamberlain was driven out of office in 1940, saw a role for the BBC in wartime and had wanted it closed down. Chamberlain thought that people 'would not have time to listen to the radio'. This survives as one of the war's great ironies, for

Prime Minister Neville
Chamberlain waves the
document promising
'peace in our time'
after his 1938 meeting
with Hitler in Munich.

The first intimation that the people of
Britain received that war really was unavoidable
came not so much with the invasion of Poland
but with the response of the BBC. Radio
output had until then been divided into two
networks, the national service and the regional
service. The fear in government was that the
network of transmitters used for the regional
service would act as a series of navigation
beacons for enemy aircraft. Therefore, on the
day Hitler swept into Poland, the BBC closed
down its two networks and replaced them
with one, the Home Service. On the same day,
the television service was closed altogether.
Also on 1 September, the evacuation from
London of more than one million children
began and a sunset-to-sunrise blackout was
imposed on the capital. Two days
later, on Sunday 3 September, Britain
declared war on Germany. At 11.15
a.m., Chamberlain broadcast: 'I am
speaking to you from the Cabinet
Room at Number 10 Downing
Street. This morning the British
Ambassador in Berlin handed the
German government a final note
stating that, unless the British
government heard from them by 1
1 o'clock that they were prepared at
once to withdraw their troops from
Poland, a state of war would exist
between us.' Then came the fateful
words that were to send a chill
through everyone listening, most of
them having hoped against hope
that this moment could somehow

be avoided: 'I have to tell you now that no such
undertaking has been received and that conse-
quently this country is at war with Germany…'

Chamberlain's broadcast lasted five minutes.
Eight minutes later air raid sirens sounded in
London and people rushed for the streets and
the shelters. This was absurd; Hitler had not
expected a declaration of war so soon after
the invasion of Poland so there was not the
slightest possibility that his bombers could be
over London. Other absurdities were to follow.
In a positive orgy of self-denial, Britain closed
down its cinemas, theatres, football clubs and all
other places of entertainment. Given the policy
that was put into effect at Broadcasting House,
albeit for a mercifully brief time, a good many
listeners were to wish that the BBC had closed

down. The war was to be the making of the BBC's reputation, assisted by newsprint rationing which curtailed the activities of the newspapers. But first both the Corporation and its listeners – more than nine million radio licences were issued in 1939 alone – had to overcome what might be called Sandy Macpherson syndrome. Macpherson was an organist. Because the government anticipated an immediate assault by Hitler, the BBC schedules were pared to the bone. The stipulation that it could not broadcast news bulletins before 7 p.m., a sop to the newspaper proprietors, was at last lifted. From not enough news, there was now to be almost nothing but news. And Sandy Macpherson. The news, the *Daily Service* and *Children's Hour* were the sole survivors from the pre-war schedule. Government ministers traipsed in and out of Broadcasting House to give long and often tedious dissertations about everything from evacuation procedures to food rationing. Talks carried titles such as 'Making the Most of a Wartime Larder'. The nation was being lectured, pampered and patronized and the nation was soon fed up with it.

In between the talks and the bulletins, records were played and Macpherson pounded away at the organ. The man was doing his best, indeed he was an accomplished musician. Listeners were unimpressed; several wrote to the BBC and to *Radio Times*, saying that they would cheerfully face the Germans if it meant escaping from Macpherson. The press, already critical of the fact that many BBC staff had been moved out of London, now opened a second front in its war with the BBC. 'For God's sake' said the *Sunday Pictorial*, 'how long is the BBC to be allowed to broadcast its travesty of a programme which goes under the name of entertainment?'

The answer was: not much longer. Within days of the war starting, variety was back on the air (a show starring Tommy Handley) and drama and classical music returned to the schedules in October. The so-called phoney war was still going on and there was little hard news to report: the aircraft carrier HMS *Courageous* was torpedoed in the Bristol Channel on 17 September and Britain lost a score of merchant ships in the first two weeks

(Left) The London Underground served a useful purpose as the world's largest bomb shelter and thousands slept 'down below' as the blitz continued. (Right) The cover of *Radio Times* that featured first-hand accounts of young evacuees.

of the war. Nonetheless, there were few major developments until Hitler swept through Norway, Denmark, the Netherlands and France in the spring of 1940, eventually trapping the ill-starred British Expeditionary Force (BEF) on the beaches of Dunkirk, from which the famous 'little ship' evacuation was to take place. In seven months, Britain had moved from worrying about too much organ music on the radio to facing an enemy camped 30 miles across the Channel. France surrendered on 17 June 1940, a moment Godfrey Talbot, a news sub-editor when the war started and who went on to become one of the campaign's finest correspondents, remembers well: 'The word got around Broadcasting House that this terrible thing had happened, the French had given up. I was conscious of people coming and standing behind my shoulder and you could hear the swift intake of breath as they read what I was dictating.'

The war was to have several distinct, though in some cases overlapping, phases. First came the blitzkrieg launched by Hitler's bombers against British cities, which was followed by the struggle for air supremacy between the RAF and the *Luftwaffe* in 1940. In 1941 came the entry of the United States into the war after the Japanese bombed Pearl Harbor. Then came the long preparations for a counter-offensive by the Allies, which reached its climax on D-Day and the surrender of the German forces the following year. This was followed by the dropping of the first atomic bombs on Hiroshima and Nagasaki, which brought the surrender of Japan. The detail of these

enormous events is not for this book but a flavour of them is to be found in the words of BBC reporters who travelled the world with the troops, and a taste of how Britain lived through the war can be found in the domestic BBC archive.

Hundreds of thousands of children were evacuated from major cities, many of them having the time of their lives after swapping housing estates for farms. Reporters regularly visited the children, partly because their experiences were inherently interesting and partly as a way of reassuring parents. Thus one BBC reporter went to a farm and asked a boy how he was getting on: 'Hello mum and dad, don't get worried about us, we're all very happy here. I don't think anybody wants to go home, yet. We go on the moors nearly every night and watch all the cows and the sheep grazing and the river flowing. Last week the boys and girls had a match of netball, and there was 14 girls and three boys. The girls won us.' These broadcasts made up in warmth what they lacked in grammatical exactitude and they proved to be an important contribution to the country's morale.

There is another set of broadcasts, this time by an adult that made an even greater impression. The broadcasts of Winston Churchill were to galvanize the nation against Hitler. Indeed, the story of the war itself, or at least of its high and low points, can be told through these speeches, some of which were written for broadcasting, others of which were broadcast versions of Churchill's speeches to Parliament. The broadcasts usually came from 10 Downing Street or Chequers, the British Prime Minister's country retreat, though a few were transmitted from the bunker underneath Downing Street. Ironically, Churchill did not think much of the BBC, having railed against its alleged bias during the 1926 General Strike. He makes no mention of the broadcasts in his memoirs but they undoubtedly served as a clarion call to a country whose people were deeply troubled by the war.

In 1940 alone, Churchill made five broadcasts of quite extraordinary effectiveness. In May: 'I have formed an administration of men and women of every party and of almost every point of view. We have differed and quarrelled in the past, but now one bond unites us all: to wage war until victory is won and never to surrender ourselves to servitude and shame, whatever the cost and the agony may be...' In early June, after the evacuation of British troops from Dunkirk:

'We shall go on to the end... we shall fight on the seas and oceans, we shall fight with growing confidence and growing strength in the air, we shall defend our island whatever the cost may be. We shall fight on the beaches, we shall fight on the landing grounds, we shall fight in the fields and in the streets...we shall never surrender.'

Britain's grim position, and Churchill's growing frustration at the lack of American help, much less involvement, is reflected in a remark attributed to Churchill, off air, after that speech: 'And we'll fight them with the butt ends of broken glass bottles, because that's all we'll bloody well have left.'

The same month, after the fall of Paris, Churchill said: 'What General de Gaulle called the Battle of France is over. I expect the Battle of Britain is about to begin. Upon this battle depends the survival of Christian civilization. Upon it depends our own British life. Though the fury and might of the enemy must very soon to be turned on us, Hitler knows that he will have to break us in this island or lose the war. Let us therefore brace ourselves to our duties and so bear ourselves that if the British Empire and its Commonwealth last for a thousand years, men will still say, "this was their finest hour".'

Churchill made a similar speech to the nation on 14 July, when the Germans had begun blanket bombing of British cities, this time with a particular message for the people of London: 'Should the invader come to Britain there will be no placid lying down of the people in submission. We shall defend every village, every town and every city.

The vast mass of London itself, fought street by street, could easily devour an entire hostile army and we would rather see London laid in ruins and ashes than that it should be tamely and abjectly enslaved.' And on 20 August, after the Battle of Britain had been won by the RAF, Churchill found another ringing phrase that would go into the lexicon of British rhetoric: 'Never in the field of human conflict was so much owed by so many to so few. All our hearts go out to the fighter pilots whose brilliant actions we see with our own eyes day after day. But we must never forget that night after night, month after month, our bomber squadrons travel far into Germany to find their

targets in the darkness by the highest navigational skill, aim their attacks, often under the heaviest fire, often with serious loss, with deliberate, careful discrimination, and inflict shattering blows upon the whole of the technical and war-making structure of the Nazi power.'

If Churchill was undoubtedly the war's star broadcaster, others who sat at microphones were also making huge reputations. The nation had an enormous thirst for war news and in the very month of the Dunkirk evacuation and the Battle of Britain, they were to be given the names of the people who brought them

**Operation Overlord:
Royal Marines come
ashore on the beaches
of Normandy on
6 June 1944 as the
D-Day invasion starts.**

the news. Until then, newsreaders had been anonymous. Certainly, they sounded anonymous, indeed they all sounded like one man. John Reith had decreed that BBC announcers should speak in unaccented southern English using what came to be called the Received Pronunciation. It was in 1940 that John Snagge, subsequently famous for his commentaries on the Boat Race, then running the Presentation department, suggested that announcers say who they were. In a remarkable bypassing of the BBC's usual let's-call-a-meeting response, the policy was instituted the next day when listeners heard the words: 'Here is the news read by Alvar Liddell'. There was a minor irritating intervention by the pedants, who said that the wording did not make it clear that the person introducing the bulletin was also the one reading it. Therefore it became: 'Here is the news and this is Alvar Liddell reading it'.

Liddell, Snagge, Frank Phillips, Alan Howland, Joseph McLeod, Freddy Allen and Bruce Belfrage became huge stars and attracted fan mail. They were the most unlikely of celebrities

and the news they had to read was, for many months, unremittingly grim. Two events in 1941 heralded change, however. Hitler made the fateful decision to tear up his treaty with Russia and open an eastern front. And Japan attacked the US at Pearl Harbor, thus bringing America into the war, both in Europe and the Pacific. American troops may not have been greeted with much enthusiasm in the pubs and music halls of Britain ('overpaid, oversexed, over here') but American manpower and armaments were as welcome to the war effort as the nylon stockings they brought with them were welcome to British girls in dance halls. By now this was truly a world war, fought in the fields of Europe, the deserts of North Africa and the jungles of the Far East.

The beginning of the end came on 6 June 1944: D-Day. The moment had been a long time in the planning. As early as 1942 more than 30,000 British people had responded to a Royal Navy request to supply their holiday snapshots of the French coast, though Normandy was not of course specified. Those long, flat beaches of northern France were about to be churned up by the largest armed force ever assembled on this planet: two million men, 10,000 trucks, 15,000 tanks, 5,300 ships, 10,000 aircraft. It was impossible to keep the fact of the invasion secret, only its precise date and the precise target: right to the last moment, Hitler thought the Allies would land at the Pas de Calais. One of the BBC's most distinguished war correspondents, Frank Gillard, quoted in Tom Hickman's *What Did You Do In The War, Auntie?*, recalled travelling by

car 100 miles across southern England: 'It was incredible. Wherever you looked, anywhere there was any kind of cover – in the hedgerows, in people's private gardens – there were military vehicles, trucks, ambulances, tanks, armoured cars, jeeps, bulldozers, Dukws (amphibious vehicles) and endless columns of soldiers. In one place there was a bit of clear ground and there were a couple of dozen Tommies (soldiers) in their uniforms and their heavy boots, having a knock-up game of cricket. I couldn't help thinking of Drake and Plymouth Hoe.'

Millions of people knew about the invasion before the BBC announced it because they had been kept awake by the noise from thousands of Allied aircraft. At 9.32 a.m. on 6 June, John Snagge broke into the scheduled programming: 'D-Day has come. Early this morning the Allies began the assault on the north-western face of Hitler's European fortress…' BBC reporters were already heading for Normandy with the troops. Richard Dimbleby flew in a Mosquito aircraft over the French beaches. Stanley Maxted and Richard North arrived on the beaches from a minesweeper and a landing craft respectively. These reporters and others broadcast direct from the beaches, via a truck with a mobile transmitter, call sign 'Mike Charlie Oboe', mounted in it. Two more mobile transmitters, in crates, were ready to be used elsewhere as the invasion went on.

The Allied advance was to be painfully slow and, as so often happens in wartime, the leaders of a bogged down army started looking for scapegoats. The BBC was one of those for

Field Marshall Montgomery, the most revered of the British commanders, who was under pressure from the political leaders to make faster progress. 'Monty', his forces held up near Caen in France, complained about details of one offensive being broadcast on the BBC news at 9 p.m. General Omar Bradley, commander of the American Twelfth Army Group, complained that a BBC broadcast had 'cost the lives of American soldiers' by giving details of an offensive at Falaise, though this was later proven to be a failure of the army censors. Frank Gillard was reporting the activities of Monty's men for the BBC but after complaints that the Americans were not getting enough mentions on the air, Gillard was switched to follow Bradley's Twelfth Army, much to the chagrin of Montgomery, who had formed a close relationship with Gillard. Montgomery was particularly impressed on one occasion when he wanted a piece of news broadcast but Gillard's transmitter lines were down. So Gillard called the War Office on Montgomery's red 'hot line' and was patched through to a BBC recording engineer in Broadcasting House.

Gillard was already established as one of the great war reporters when, on 25 April 1945, he reported one of the war's defining moments: American soldiers meeting up with their Russian allies at Torgau on the River Elbe in Germany. Gillard was there and possessed the only transmitter. American reporters wanted to share it: but who would go first? Ultimately, they tossed a coin and Gillard won. He broadcast live on the 6 p.m. news,

announcing that Russian and American soldiers had crossed the Elbe in rowing boats, their rifles reversed, and shook hands.

There had been a grislier reporting task for Richard Dimbleby on 19 April, when he entered the Belsen concentration camp with Allied soldiers. Here at last was the unvarnished proof of Hitler's evil. Dimbleby described it as 'the most horrible day of my life'. He filed a 14-minute report, which included these words: 'I wish with all my heart that everyone fighting in this war, and above all those whose duty it is to direct the war from Britain and America, could have come with me through the barbed wire fence that leads to the inner compound... the dead and dying lay close together. I picked

The BBC's war correspondent Richard Dimbleby (far left) pictured outside Hitler's underground shelter in July 1945.

my way over corpse after corpse in the gloom until I heard one voice that rose above the gentle, undulating moaning. I found a girl, she was a living skeleton, impossible to gauge her age for she had practically no hair left on her head and her face was a yellow parchment sheet with two holes in it for eyes. She was stretching out her stick of an arm and gasping something. It was 'English, English, medicine, medicine' and she was trying to cry but had not enough strength…'

That and other reports were to bring home to people in Britain and America the full extent of the horror that had been inflicted by the Nazis. Those reports also demonstrated what the war had been about, something that needed to be done given the weary state of the British nation, many of its cities reduced to rubble, hundreds of thousands of its young men either dead or in prison camps across Europe and the Far East. At least the end was not far away.

Hitler's suicide was announced on 1 May. The BBC interrupted programmes at 7 p.m. the next day to announce the surrender of the Germans in Italy and just over three hours later there was another newsflash, announcing that Berlin had fallen to the Allies. On Monday 7 May, cheering crowds gathered outside Buckingham Palace. They knew the war in Europe was over, even if the BBC had not announced it because of an agreement that all three major Allies, the US, Britain and Russia, would make the announcement at the same time. At 7.40 p.m., the BBC interrupted programmes to say that the following day would be celebrated as Victory in Europe (VE) day. Churchill broadcast to the nation on 8 May.

On 26 July, the Allies issued an ultimatum to Japan: surrender or be crushed. Japan did not respond. The manner of its crushing was heralded in a news bulletin read by Frank Phillips on 6 August: 'Scientists, British and American, have made the atomic bomb at last…' On 9 August, the atom bomb was dropped on Hiroshima, killing 70,000 people, followed by a second bomb at Nagasaki, killing 39,000 people. On Tuesday 14 August, Japan surrendered. By that time there had been a general election in Britain, bringing a landslide victory for Labour, which had used a clever slogan: 'Cheer Churchill, Vote Labour'. So it was the new Prime Minister, Clement Attlee, who broadcast to the nation at midnight that day. Most people were in bed.

Next day, Wednesday 15 August, King George VI said in a radio broadcast: 'From the bottom of my heart, I thank my peoples for all they have done, not only for themselves, but for mankind'. World War II was over.

The King is Dead. Long Live the Queen 1952

Death of King George VI heralds start of second Elizabethan age

The new Queen arrives home from Kenya to be greeted by (from right) Winston Churchill, the Prime Minister; Clement Atlee, leader of the Labour Party; Anthony Eden, Foreign Secretary; and Lord Woolton, Lord President of the Council.

THE PHRASE 'A NATION MOURNS' has appeared in nearly every newspaper after the death of nearly every monarch to the point where it has become a cliché. In the late twentieth century, the death of a British monarch might be expected to be greeted with more equivocation, given that republican impulses are now much stronger than at any time in the past. However, in 1952, when King George VI died, a sense of loss pervaded virtually the entire population. King George was a much-respected monarch, a diffident man who had come to the throne reluctantly and unexpectedly as a consequence of the abdication crisis of 1936. King George had heard the call of duty and responded to it. He led the country in war and peace, earning huge affection, in particular, for the royal family's refusal to move out of London during the blitz: 'We could never look the East End in the face again,' Queen Elizabeth (now the Queen Mother) said at the time. King George was only 56 when he died. He had been suffering from lung cancer for several years and he died of a thrombosis at Sandringham House in the early

hours of 6 February 1952. His relative youth added to the sense of loss. The nation mourned. It was to prove the end of the era of austerity and diffidence towards the royal family. The change in attitude would not surface for some years, but the coming of the second Elizabethan age would undoubtedly herald different attitudes on the part of an enriched and emboldened population.

If the death of King George was expected given the nature of the King's illness, its timing was a shock. Princess Elizabeth and her husband, the Duke of Edinburgh, had flown out of Britain only a week before for a holiday at the Treetops Hotel in Kenya and the King had seen them off from the tarmac at Heathrow Airport, where he stood hatless in a freezing wind. Winston Churchill, who was now in 10 Downing Street for a second spell as Prime Minister, recalled later that the King must have known he did not have long to live; he was, Churchill said, 'walking with death'. In the British way of things, the succession was immediate. Indeed Elizabeth was Queen before she knew it. She was sitting on a platform built into a

giant fig tree outside Treetops on the morning that the King died, photographing animals. Jim Corbett, a near-legendary 'white hunter', stood at the base of the tree carrying a rifle. His nominal purpose was to protect the royal princess from wild animals but there were human risks too: Mau Mau terrorists were known to be active in the area.

A few minutes after breakfast at Treetops, Elizabeth and Philip returned to Sagana Lodge, which had been given to the couple as a wedding present (in 1947) by the people of Kenya. The couple began preparing for a trip to Mombassa, from where they were due to embark on the SS *Gothic* to travel to

Australasia. Still news of her father's death had not reached Elizabeth. The reason for the delay was to be found in London, at two different locations: Buckingham Palace and the BBC. A telegram was supposed to have been despatched from the Palace to Kenya announcing the death. There is no universal agreement as to why this telegram was not sent but the King's assistant private secretary, Sir Edward Ford, told Sarah Bradford for her biography of Elizabeth that the code term for the death of the King – Hyde Park Corner – was misunderstood by the telegraphists: they thought it was the address, not the message. The BBC delayed the announcement because the powers that were decided that only John Snagge had a voice of sufficient gravitas to make it and he could not be found. It was indeed Snagge who eventually broke the news: 'This is London. It is with the greatest sorrow that we make the following announcement. It was announced from Sandringham at 10.45 today that the King, who retired to rest last night in his usual health, passed peacefully away in his sleep early this morning. The BBC offers profound sympathy to Her Majesty the Queen and the royal family.'

Frank Gillard was the BBC's man with the royal party in Kenya and he sent a graphic report from Nairobi, giving poignant context to the news: 'How tragic to think that even as she was on the veranda at Treetops, looking out on the wild animals of Africa, going about their strange ways in the moonlight, that at such a moment she should become Queen… even this morning, as she sat at breakfast, talking about her father and proudly describing how bravely he'd stood up to his illness and how well he'd recovered, sitting there in her yellow bush shirt and brown slacks, even at that moment her father was lying dead and she had succeeded to his vast responsibilities.' Elizabeth was told of her father's death by the duke, who had been taken on one side by an equerry once the news finally arrived from England. Elizabeth, given the news at 2.45 p.m. in Kenya, 10.45 a.m. in London, reportedly took it 'calmly', a response that at once reflected her upbringing and indicated the quiet calm that she would bring to her new role, thrust upon her at the age of 25. Martin Charteris, the new queen's

private secretary, went to see Elizabeth a few minutes after she had heard the news. He said she was slightly flushed but otherwise calm; she was sitting at a desk, writing letters of apology about the cancellation of her tour to Australasia. Charteris asked what she would call herself as Queen: 'My own name of course, what else?' Elizabeth replied. Clearly, the new queen had grasped her destiny with the firmest of hands.

Less than three hours later, a car took the Queen along dusty roads to the township of Nanyuki, which has few claims to fame apart from the fact that it sits directly on the equator. Elizabeth had been due to visit Nanyuki the following day and as officials heard of the King's death they hastily took down the bunting that adorned the streets. The Union flag could not, however, be flown at half-mast because it had been nailed to the flagpole. The Queen was driven through the town to the local airfield, whose manager was anxious; darkness was approaching and he did not want to light the runway with flares for fear of starting a bush fire. Gillard watched as the Queen, in a beige dress with a white hat, mounted the aircraft's steps. She had taken no mourning clothes to Treetops, where space was limited, but suitable clothing was being flown from Mombassa to meet the plane at Entebbe. She walked up the gangway of the Dakota that would fly her home, and at 6.57 p.m. local time the aircraft took off.

When it arrived at Heathrow there was a scene that would go into the photographic annals of history. A young woman, the new queen, walked down the steps of the aircraft to be greeted at the bottom by a line of elderly men, now her subjects. The Queen was dressed entirely in black, as were the men. The Queen was wearing a black hat, the men, as was the custom, were hatless. The men were from the highest reaches of government, except for one who was leader of the Labour Opposition. They were Churchill, Clement Attlee, Anthony Eden and Lord Woolton. Churchill greeted the Queen first, but was so overcome with the emotion of the occasion that he could hardly find words.

There is a widespread notion that the British establishment moves ponderously but this is to confuse appearance with reality. In fact, the changing of one monarch for another is carried out using procedures that have been tested down the centuries, but never to destruction. On this occasion there was a brutal swiftness about the procedure that the Queen herself would have understood well but which seemed chilling from the outside. On the morning of 8 February, a dozen hours after the Queen landed at Heathrow and only 36 hours after the King had died, the Accession Council met in St James's Palace. The Queen entered the room to meet her Privy Council and to read out the formal Declaration of Sovereignty. At the end the Queen said: 'My heart is too full for me to say more to you today than that I shall always work as my father did'. The Duke of Edinburgh stepped forward and led the Queen away. They got into a car. On the ramparts of St James's Palace, the Garter King of Arms proclaimed the succession for all to hear:

'Queen Elizabeth the Second, by the grace of God, Queen of this realm and of all her other realms and territories, Head of the Commonwealth, Defender of the Faith…' As the words rang out the Queen's car drove away and, for the first time, the Queen wept.

That afternoon she went to Sandringham, where her father's body lay. The numbing grief that enveloped the house was almost visible. The Queen was to write, much later, about a key difference in the burden her mother and her sister, Princess Margaret, had to bear compared with her own: 'Mummy and Margaret have the biggest grief to bear for their future must seem very blank, while I have a job and a family to think of'. Once the King's funeral was over the nation could start preparing for the Queen's coronation. It would be a joyous occasion, certainly the most

colourful event in Britain for a very long time. After the ravages of war and the austerity imposed by post-war rationing, the country needed a party and this was a better excuse than most. The death of a King may be sad, but the accession of a beautiful young princess to the throne was an event worth shouting about. Britain was ready to look kindly upon the new Queen Elizabeth, not only because of her youth and beauty but also because she had endeared herself to the nation during the war. She had broadcast messages of support and had donned uniform, working as a mechanic on army vehicles. Given some of the criticism she would attract much later, it was ironic that Elizabeth, in her younger days, was seen as the people's princess, a sobriquet subsequently attached to Diana, Princess of Wales.

The coronation at Westminster Abbey broke new ground as a public spectacle. Coronations have a thousand-year history in Britain but this was the first to be broadcast around the world, for by now television was sufficiently established to enable it to give the public unique access to great events. If television was the making of the coronation, the reverse was also true, for the coming of the coronation prompted an unprecedented increase in sales of television sets. The event was the making of the medium, yet it very nearly did not happen as a television spectacle: the first decision of the Coronation Commission, chaired by Prince Philip, was to cause uproar. It announced that television would be banned from the abbey. Instead, a documentary film would be made of selected

parts of the ceremony and the BBC would be allowed to show this at a later date. Churchill and the Conservative cabinet endorsed this plan, Churchill believing that televising the event would place too great a strain on the Queen. The Archbishop of Canterbury and the rest of the abbey clergy were also opposed to television, believing that allowing people to watch the ceremony in their homes somehow detracted from the dignity of the occasion.

What did the Queen feel? Most Royal historians believe that she initially took the side of the traditionalists, changing her mind only when the newspapers launched a campaign to get the event televised. Sir Alexander Cadogan, the shrewd chairman of the BBC, evidently decided to keep his powder dry: 'I think that we can leave it to an enraged public opinion to bring pressure on the government' he said. Within days of the announcement the retreat was sounded and a compromise worked out; television would film everything except the most private and sacred moment of the ceremony, the communion.

There was also a long debate about when the coronation should take place. The British economy was still fragile at the time of King George's death and Churchill was determined that no working days should be lost. That, together with the fact that the abbey was being extensively restored, ruled out a coronation in 1952. So the thoughts of the Coronation Commission turned to 1953. They briefly considered 3 June until it was realized that that would clash with the running of the Derby at Epsom; the Queen, already a horse racing

enthusiast (as was Churchill), readily accepted that the clash would be unthinkable. There were those who favoured 1 June, a Monday, but – and this was a sign of the times – it was realized that having the coronation on a Monday would involve a great deal of Sunday travelling, which might offend those who honoured the Sabbath as a day of rest. So Tuesday 2 June was chosen. The day would be declared a national bank holiday.

In the event Prince Philip was to prove a modernizer and that, plus his reputation, then as now, for plain speaking meant that there were some lively meetings of the Coronation Commission. The deputy chairman was the Duke of Norfolk, a man of no great education who was bluff, deeply conservative and very much a man of the turf. The snobbery of the racing fraternity in those days was well illustrated by the story of a peer of the realm who, being a divorcee, was afraid he might not get an invitation to the coronation. 'Good God man' the Duke of Norfolk told him, 'this is a coronation, not Royal Ascot'.

Coronation day itself was to provide proof that, whatever problems the British may have had, they had not lost their touch when it came to organizing great events. The coronation was a spectacle and it was spectacular. Millions of people thronged central London, they lined the route, hung from windows, clambered on to rooftops. At least one million people were in place by the Sunday night, two days before the ceremony. This being Britain in May, it rained and it was chilly. But the crowds were undaunted. There was a sense of a great national coming together, a wish on the part of ordinary people to use the occasion as a reason to close ranks, and thus to say something collectively about the values that bound the nation.

On television there was a British audience of 20 million, but that was increased at least tenfold by viewers in Europe, the Commonwealth and elsewhere: 80 million people in America watched a recording of the ceremony. Richard Dimbleby was the main commentator, indeed Dimbleby had been influential in bringing about the change of mind over televising the ceremony. The atmosphere was made all the more carnival-like by the rapid improvement in economic prospects, even compared with the previous year. This was somewhat illusory, for although people had more money to spend Britain's share of world trade was diminishing. But there was a sense of hope and optimism to which the new queen gave a new focus. A leading article in *The Times* on the morning of the ceremony said: 'Having made service her career, she has the reward of

the selfless in the pure joy of duty amply, generously, done'.

The Queen travelled from Buckingham Palace to the abbey, through drizzle, and walked slowly down the main aisle towards the altar. Descriptions at the time vary; for some she was a 'radiant young monarch', for others she 'looked pale and tender', others again saw in her face 'the strain of the occasion'. All these descriptions and others were probably accurate. The service itself was a somewhat bizarre ritual, unchanged down the centuries and having a sense of the Middle Ages about it. The Queen sat on the Coronation Chair and the Archbishop of Canterbury made this opening declaration to his fellow bishops: 'Sirs, I here present unto you Queen Elizabeth, your undoubted Queen'. A canopy was placed over the Queen's head, hiding her from the view of the congregation and the television cameras. The Archbishop made the sign of the cross over the Queen's hands, chest and head and then spoke the words that must have sounded other-worldly to most of the listening millions: 'Be thy head anointed with holy oil: as kings, priests and prophets were anointed and as Solomon was anointed King by Zadok the priest and Nathan the prophet, so be thou anointed, blessed and consecrated Queen over the Peoples, whom the Lord thy God hath given thee to rule and govern…' Then came the crowning, followed by the acclamation: 'God save Queen Elizabeth! Long live Queen Elizabeth! May the Queen live for ever!'

After the ceremony the Queen returned to her coach and thence to Buckingham Palace, accompanied by 13,000 soldiers, 29 military bands and 27 carriages, but accompanied most of all by a huge and continuous roar from the crowds along the seven-mile route (specially extended to give the maximum number of people the chance to see the procession), a roar of almost startling passion. The crowds were not to disperse for a long time, nor would the celebrations elsewhere end. There were parties all over the country, there were banquets, exhibitions and displays. An opera, *Gloriana*, specially written by

The stories were true and they immediately raised the spectre of the abdication crisis 17 years earlier, in which Edward VIII had given up the throne for a divorced woman.

There was no real comparison, for Margaret was hardly likely to ascend the throne and neither Margaret nor Townsend was married. Nonetheless, in the climate of the time, this had the smack of sensation. Townsend, who was rapidly exiled to a non-job in Brussels, became something of a national hero, with newspaper polls showing overwhelming support for the marriage. The scandal, if such it was, rumbled on long into 1954. The establishment view was

Benjamin Britten, was performed at Covent Garden in front of the Queen.

There had been a moment at the abbey, a fleeting moment involving a tiny gesture, that was to spark the first Royal controversy of the new reign but by no means the last one. In one of the abbey's ante-rooms, Princess Margaret had been seen to brush something from the lapel of her friend, Group Captain Peter Townsend. It had the appearance of an intimate gesture and tended to confirm rumours of a romance. New York newspapers ran a story the next day but it was nearly a fortnight before anything broke in Britain. The *People*, a Sunday tabloid, carried a story saying that foreign newspapers had reported Princess Margaret as being 'in love with a divorced man'.

distilled in a leading article in *The Times* on 26 October of that year: 'If the marriage which is now being discussed comes to pass…the princess will be entering into a union which vast numbers of her sister's people, all sincerely anxious for her lifelong happiness, cannot in conscience regard as a marriage'. That leader is said to have been decisive in bringing Townsend and the princess to a decision. Five days later, on 31 October, Princess Margaret issued a statement saying that she would not marry Townsend, being 'mindful of the Church's teachings that Christian marriage is indissoluble and conscious of my duty to the Common-wealth'. The second Elizabethan era had begun with a precursor of the scandals which were to bedevil its succeeding generation.

The Suez Crisis 1956

Suez invasion – the last adventure of Britain's colonial era

President Nasser warns Britain not to interfere after he had nationalized the Suez Canal.

THE LAST THING MOST BRITISH people wanted in the mid-1950s was another war, but on 26 July 1956 they woke up to discover that the last thing they wanted was the next thing they were likely to get. On that day, radio bulletins were dominated by the news that Colonel Gamal Abdul Nasser, the President of Egypt, had nationalized the Suez Canal, one of the most important waterways, as far as Western interests were concerned, in the world. He planned to impose a toll on every ship that passed through it. Nasser's move would quickly develop into an international crisis, but its real importance was in signalling the beginning of the end for the old British Empire. Suez was to become a messy, embarrassing venture which would harm Britain's reputation and end the career of one of its most distinguished politicians.

The Suez Canal was and is a 103-mile waterway through the desert, linking the Red Sea with the Mediterranean. Its construction was a stupendous feat of engineering and its economic importance could hardly be

overstated. It reduced the length of the journey made by tankers carrying oil from the Gulf states to Europe by so much that the saving quickly became built into the economics of oil supply, thus enabling petrol prices at the pump to be kept low. But one misconception about the canal was to muddle the situation in 1956 and indeed cause misunderstandings about the crisis in the years that followed. Although the Suez Canal Company was an Anglo-French operation, the land through which the canal had been dug continued to be owned by Egypt: it was leased to the company. There was to be much ranting against Nasser as the crisis wore on, much of it about the legalities of nationalization, but there is not much doubt that Nasser acted technically within his rights.

Nasser, who had led the military coup which deposed King Farouk four years earlier, was a charismatic figure within Egypt. Shortly after taking power he made it clear that, if Egypt were to grow and prosper, it would need to get more land under cultivation. To do that, a high dam would be built at Aswan on the Nile.

Nasser saw no reason why the British and the Americans should not finance the Aswan project and there were many politicians and economists in both countries who agreed with him. But there were other, more powerful voices, as it turned out, who believed that the project was ill conceived and too expensive. The Egyptian economy was weak and could not, according to Western experts, afford the Aswan project, even with Western loans and grants. It is also important to remember that Nasser was not trusted. He had developed a relationship with the Soviet Union and, earlier in 1956, the West had learned that he had done a secret deal with Moscow to buy arms worth $200 million. This purchase was underwritten by mortgaging Egypt's cotton crop, one of the staples of its economy, for some years to come.

If Nasser was not trusted in the West, he knew how to gain the trust of his own people. The manner of the Suez Canal announcement illustrated his ability to win the support of Egyptians. He made the announcement during a speech at Alexandria on the fourth anniversary of his taking power. Nasser used classical Arabic for formal speeches but on this occasion he switched to the vernacular Arabic of the streets. In so doing he made himself appear a man of the people and his rhetoric inflamed the hatred towards imperial powers such as Britain and France that ordinary Arabs had felt for generations. These powers would not like the nationalization of the canal, Nasser said, but they could 'choke to death on their fury'. He warned employees of the Suez Canal

Company, many of whom were British and French engineers, that they would be thrown into jail if they tried to leave their jobs. He expected them to carry on with business as usual.

Tens of thousands of Egyptians heard Nasser's speech, and they cheered him to the echo. He told them that the revenue from the Suez Canal toll would finance the building of the Aswan dam. The project would increase the amount of cultivated land in Egypt by more than 50 per cent and the country would also benefit by using the dam to produce cheap hydro-electricity. 'We shall industrialize Egypt and compete with the West,' Nasser said. 'We are marching from strength to strength.' While Nasser spoke in Alexandria, a cordon of riot police surrounded the Cairo headquarters of the Suez Canal Company. Nasser did offer some olive branches: he promised that shareholders in the company would be compensated and that there would be no interference with ships passing through the canal.

In London the British government was unimpressed with these assurances. Sir Anthony Eden, the Prime Minister, said that 'A man with Colonel Nasser's record cannot be allowed to have his thumb on our windpipe'. Eden's hard-line stance was to be crucial in the days and months ahead. Eden had seen what appease-

Suez caused huge
divisions of opinion in
Britain, exemplified
by this protest in
Trafalgar Square,
London.

British intent. It would not be enough to change Nasser's mind. There were many in Eden's circle who thought from the start that only troops could take back the canal, but this was by no means a universal view. Certainly, it was not the view across the Atlantic in Washington. Although the United States had condemned Nasser's move soon after it happened, later statements from John Foster Dulles, the US Secretary of State, were much more conciliatory and explicitly warned against armed intervention.

During August diplomatic and military options moved forward simultaneously, but not quite in tandem. It was noticeable that Britain and France stood together, but alone, sounding bellicose. France's particular interest in teaching Nasser a lesson arose from its belief that he was the ringmaster in Algeria, the French colony where a bloody civil war

ment could do during the Munich crisis; Nasser was not going to be Eden's Hitler. Indeed many historians believe that Eden's determination not to look like an appeaser led to the invasion at Suez and the ignominy that was heaped on Britain thereafter. Less than 48 hours after the nationalization of the canal all Egyptian assets held in Britain were frozen, though Eden knew that such a move would only send a signal of

was being fought. On 8 August Eden broadcast to the British people, a statement most noticeable for the fact that he said nothing that aimed at conciliation. Indeed, he said that 'Colonel Nasser cannot be trusted' and he hinted that the use of force could not be ruled out. A Royal Proclamation calling up reservists was issued and companies running holiday flights were asked to put 100 aircraft at

the disposal of the government to carry troops to the Middle East. Extra British forces began leaving for Cyprus in the eastern Mediterranean and the aircraft carrier *Theseus* sailed from Portsmouth, carrying the 16th Parachute Brigade.

The diplomatic offensive brought the opening, on 12 August, of the Suez conference in London, involving 22 countries which accounted for almost all the traffic through the canal. Dulles brought a proposal to the conference, which would have involved Nasser agreeing to the Suez Canal being run by an international board under the aegis of the United Nations. Eden was not very keen on this plan; he felt it represented too much of a compromise, but on 23 August the conference ended by agreeing to send Sir Robert Menzies, the Australian Prime Minister, to Cairo to see if Nasser would agree to international control. Nasser would not. Negotiations went on for over a month without any progress. Dulles continued to be vehemently opposed to armed intervention, whereas the British and French line in favour of an armed response seemed to be hardening.

Ordinary Britons had their attention diverted in September when rock'n'roll arrived on their shores in the form of the Bill Haley film *Rock Around the Clock*. The film provoked rioting in cinemas around the country involving a new phenomenon, Teddy Boys: youths with swept-back hair and sideburns wearing Edwardian-style frock coats. The anomaly of a government preparing to fight an old-fashioned colonial war in distant parts while the youth of its country jived in the aisles of cinemas seems to have been lost on social commentators of the time, but it stands out as a stark contrast now. There was a much more serious diversion in late October when the Hungarian people rose against their Soviet oppressors only to have their hopes of freedom brutally crushed by the arrival of Russian tanks on the streets of Budapest. Several thousand people, armed only with flags, died as their uprising was crushed.

If the Soviet empire was giving trouble, Britain had little reason to gloat. Its own colonial attitudes were at the root of the Suez misadventure, which now moved inexorably towards its climax. Exactly what role, if any, Israel played in the pre-planning of the Suez invasion is debated to this day, but the facts are

that on 29 October Israeli forces crossed the border with Egypt and took the Sinai Peninsula, moving to within 30 miles of the canal. Israel claimed to be acting in reprisal for Egyptian raids into its territory. In London, Eden called a cabinet meeting. In Washington, Dulles warned Israel not to start hostilities. Two days later,

On 31 October, Vickers Valiant and Canberra jets of the Royal Air Force took off from Cyprus and bombed military targets in the Suez Canal zone. In the run-up to these raids, the BBC's Arabic service had broadcast warnings to civilians to stay away from military installations.

Britain and France had, 12 hours earlier, issued an ultimatum to both Israel and Egypt to withdraw their forces from the area. Neither did. So the pretext for the Anglo-French action was that Israel's invasion represented a threat to the continued use of the canal.

American officials reacted with fury and the raids brought Anglo-American relations to their lowest point in many years. Eden's dealing in semantics did not help the situation. The words he used to describe the conflict did not hide its impact. Thus Eden told the House of Commons on 1 November: 'We are in an armed conflict. That is the phrase I have used. There has been no declaration of war.' If this was not a war it had all of the characteristics of one. On the afternoon of 6 November, British Royal Marines landed from helicopters outside Port Said and fought their way into the centre of the town. There was fierce house-to-house fighting both there and in Port Fuad, where French commandos landed and began moving south. The Egyptians were using Russian tanks and 100mm guns and General Sir Charles Keightley, the Allied Commander-in-Chief, described the fighting as 'tough', although RAF crew reported that many Egyptian soldiers had fled when they saw the paratroopers, who quickly took control of the military airfield outside Port Said. The night of 5 November

had brought a bizarre episode in which the Egyptian governor of Port Said announced that he was surrendering the town, only to change his mind the following morning after instructions were received from Cairo.

The following day was to be pivotal in the Suez crisis. It was election day in America and Dwight D Eisenhower was returned for a second term in the White House. The coming of the election was one of the reasons why Eisenhower had been so opposed to giving American support for the Suez invasion. There was little chance that the domestic American audience would have the slightest sympathy for a military campaign that increasingly smacked of a colonial power trying to have its last hurrah in the Middle East. After Eisenhower had voted near his Pennsylvania home that day, he telephoned Eden using the submarine telecommunications link that had recently opened. That morning the British cabinet had reluctantly and with some dissenting voices approved a ceasefire plan, one that had been more or less imposed by the United Nations. Eisenhower was greatly relieved at this development: 'I can't tell you how pleased we are that you found it possible to accept the ceasefire' he told Eden, who replied: 'We have taken a certain risk, but I think it was justified'. These rather cool exchanges took place at teatime, a few minutes before Eden was due to face the House of Commons. The trepidation he felt about his reception in the Commons was amply conveyed in his last words to Eisenhower over the telephone:

'If I survive here tonight, I will call you tomorrow'. There had been uproar in the Commons several times in the preceding weeks, with sittings having to be suspended while order was restored.

Eden began his address to the Commons shortly after 6 p.m. His announcement that the government had told the United Nations that it would cease military operations brought a loud shout of approval from the Labour opposition, which had vociferously opposed the entire project. Labour had, in particular, called for the whole issue to be put before the UN as soon as Nasser nationalized the canal. To Eden's partial relief, there was also cheering from the Tory benches, though by no means all of the Conservative MPs joined in. Eden also continued with his insistence that the Anglo-French intervention had been a peacekeeping move aimed at keeping the Israelis in check, thus maintaining the official story that Britain and France had not colluded with Israel. Eden told the Commons: 'I do not think that anybody who has followed the military story

of recent days can have the least doubt that had the Israeli forces so wished they could have gone very much further forward than they in effect did'.

With the ceasefire soon to be implemented, attention turned away from the nuts and bolts of the withdrawal from Suez and towards the more important issues. This had never been a conflict whose outcome was dependent on the military, which could easily have overrun Egypt. The conflict, and particularly its resolution, was really about politics and economics. Long before Selwyn Lloyd, the British Foreign Secretary, went before a hostile United Nations later in November, still claiming that Britain had succeeded in 'stopping a small war', it was apparent that the United States had put the financial screws on Harold Macmillan, Britain's Chancellor (and Eden's successor). Soon after the military action at Suez had begun, international currency markets began a run on the pound that quickly turned into a sterling crisis. Macmillan, who had been one of the

(Below) It took many months to clear the canal of ships that had been scuttled by the Egyptians to block the waterway.

(Right) Tens of thousands of Egyptians greeted President Nasser's car after the British and French withdrawal from Suez.

strongest advocates of invasion when Nasser seized the canal, returned from meetings with US Treasury officials having changed his mind. The message from the Americans had been blunt: if you want us to run a support operation for the pound, you will have to deliver a ceasefire in Suez.

Macmillan reported this to a British cabinet meeting, together with the news that, during the first week of November, Britain had used up a fifth of its reserves in supporting sterling. If the reserves were a casualty of Suez, Eden was another. On 19 November Downing Street issued a statement saying that Eden was suffering from what was described as 'severe overstrain' and that he would therefore be leaving immediately for Jamaica and three weeks' rest. Eden was a suave, charming man with the appearance of a 1930s matinée idol,

but he had not been well for several years (he had three major operations in 1953, before he became Prime Minister). Towards the end of the Suez crisis his normally even temperament had given way to moody behaviour and uncharacteristic outbursts at colleagues. His departure for Jamaica effectively marked the end of his political career. RA (Rab) Butler took over as acting Prime Minister. Butler, forever the bridesmaid, never the bride, again failed to secure the top job when Eden resigned in January 1957 and he was replaced by Macmillan after a Machiavellian procedure that typified higher Tory politics in those days.

With the troops withdrawn from Suez and the crisis over, Macmillan set about repairing the so-called 'special relationship' with the United States. In this he succeeded spectacularly well, building a good relationship with Eisenhower and an even better one with John F Kennedy, who became President in 1960. By then there had been a fundamental shift in the balance of power relating to the Middle East, partly born of Britain's recognition that it was no longer economically powerful enough to be a world power and partly brought about by

America's willingness to fill the vacuum. America would now become the world's policeman and there would be no more British 'lone wolf' operations. Macmillan crystallized the change in Britain's outlook during a famous speech in Cape Town on 3 February 1960: 'The wind of change is blowing through this continent and, whether we like it or not, this growth of national consciousness is a political fact.' He was referring specifically to Africa, but the implication for Britain's colonial policy as a whole was plain. However, the process of giving Britain a more realistic role in the world had begun long before that speech and not long after Suez. In 1957 Britain's Ministry of Defence produced a White Paper which announced that National Service, under which all able-bodied young men spent two years in the armed forces, would be ended. Britain would henceforth cut its cloth according to its needs and abilities.

The final irony of the Suez crisis was that a canal Britain and France had been prepared to fight for in 1956 would shortly lose much of its economic significance. Eleven years after Suez came the 1967 war between Egypt and Israel, which brought about the bombing and closure of the Suez Canal. What would have been a catastrophe for the West a decade earlier now became a minor inconvenience, for by then supertankers had been developed which made carrying oil via the long sea route from the Middle East via the Cape of Good Hope a viable proposition. And the Aswan High Dam? It was built, using money borrowed from the Russians. The dam had been completed, but was not yet operational when Nasser died, aged only 52, in 1970, after a series of illnesses — he had circulatory problems, and was a diabetic. Eden, having become Lord Avon, enjoyed a peaceful retirement and died in 1977.

The Munich Air Crash 1958

Eight young Manchester United stars killed in Munich air disaster

CAPTAIN JAMES THAIN HAD FLOWN the twin-engine charter jet to Belgrade, carrying Manchester United's young team to their European Cup quarter-final against Red Star. Now, on the return journey, Thain had switched to the right-hand seat, handing control of the aircraft to his co-pilot, Captain Kenneth Rayment. The aircraft had flown from Belgrade to Munich, where it had stopped to refuel, and now it was ready for the final homeward leg. It was just after lunchtime on 6 February 1958. As the aircraft accelerated down the runway, the port engine pressure gauge began to fluctuate. The take-off was aborted. The problem was a 'boost surge', in which the fuel mixture became too rich, causing a surge in power. The problem had occurred in these aircraft before, especially at higher altitude airports such as Munich. There was no real danger; in fact the aircraft was capable of getting airborne on one engine.

The second attempt to take off was aborted after 40 seconds. There was an imbalance in the pressure between the two engines. Rayment told the passengers there was a technical fault while Thain taxied the plane back to the airport buildings. It had been snowing and although the runways had been cleared, the grass areas between them were still covered with snow. An engineer came to the aircraft, expressed no particular concern about boost surging, discussed re-tuning the engines (which would have meant an overnight stop) but decided that there was no need. The two captains decided on a third take-off attempt, but were delayed because the

The tangled wreckage of the Elizabethan airliner after it slewed off the runway at Munich.

MATT BUSBY
Manchester United Manager
on

DUNCAN
EDWARDS

British soccer's No. 1
hope for the future

(Left) Duncan Edwards was one of the youngest and probably the most promising of the Busby Babes. (Right) Manchester United line up before the game against Red Star, the last time they would play together.

passengers had disembarked. They were duly found and at three minutes past 3 p.m. the Elizabethan started rolling down Runway 24/25. The German air accident inquiry report said: 'The last message from 609 Zulu Uniform starts with a howling, whistling noise and ends with a loud background noise after the message was broken off.'

Thain recalled that he registered a sudden drop in the air speed indicator, followed a few seconds later by Rayment shouting: 'Christ, we can't make it'. Thain looked up from the instruments and saw what Rayment had already seen: the aircraft was heading towards a house and a tree. Inside the house, Mrs Anna Winkler was sewing. When the plane hit, she threw two of her sleeping children out into the snow and the other two crawled out through a window. The aircraft spun as it hit the house, and the branches of the tree pierced the side of the flight deck where Rayment was sitting. He died instantly. The other side of the plane, the starboard side, crashed into a hut. Beside

the hut was a parked lorry, which exploded on impact. During the two aborted take-offs, most of the players had been relaxed, playing cards and celebrating their arrival in the European Cup semi-final, where they were confident of beating Real Madrid. The cards had been put away for the third attempt. Most of the players were anxious by then. A couple of minutes later, when the aircraft finally came to a halt, the cream of British football lay dead in the wreckage. The Busby Babes were no more.

Seven of the players were killed instantly and the teenage wing-half Duncan Edwards, regarded by many as potentially the finest player ever produced in Britain, was to die later in hospital. Three members of the United staff and eight journalists, including the former England goalkeeper Frank Swift, also died. Matt Busby, the manager, lay dangerously ill in a Munich hospital. He was to recover and take United back to the top of the game, but it was to be a long haul and Busby always carried the memory of what had happened at Munich. He never discussed the crash, neither publicly nor even within his own family.

News of the crash reached a stunned British public at around 3 o'clock that afternoon, although at that stage the scale of the disaster was not known and the BBC bulletin led, somewhat optimistically, with the number of survivors. Once it became clear that many of the players, officials and reporters had died, Manchester came to a virtual standstill as workers tuned into radio sets and rushed to get copies of the *Manchester Evening News*. The BBC sent a reporter into the streets of

Manchester and the words of the people he interviewed graphically convey the scale of the shock: 'The biggest tragedy Manchester's ever had'; 'A terrible shock... I don't think they can ever be replaced, this team of very fine young men... a credit to football.' In those days Manchester was one of the great British newspaper centres, with national newspapers writing and printing northern editions with only minimum input from London. Many of the journalists who died came from the city. Indeed, when news of the crash came through, northern editors were sitting in their offices waiting for the reporters to return to write follow-up stories for that night's editions. Soon it became apparent that the reporters had become part of the story. Of course the crash has gone into history because of the players who died. They were Roger Byrne, the captain, aged 28, Tommy Taylor, aged 25, David Pegg, 22, Liam Whelan, 22, Eddie Colman, 21, Mark Jones, 24, Geoff Bent, 25. Edwards, who was only 19, died from his injuries 15 days after the crash.

The team that Busby had built had been the fulfilment of a dream. Busby had become manager of United in 1945, immediately after the war ended, when the club was in disarray. They had to play home matches on the Maine Road ground of their arch rivals, Manchester City, because United's Old Trafford headquarters had been reduced to rubble by German bombers. While the stadium was being rebuilt, Busby and his legendary assistant, Jimmy Murphy, set about the most important job of all, gathering the human resources. There were to be many ups and downs over the next few years and Busby went through one especially bad spell with some supporters calling for him to be sacked. But by the mid-1950s it was clear that Busby and Murphy had found exceptional talent in every position.

The Busby Babes also seemed to fit the mood of the time. Wartime austerity had given way to relative prosperity in the 1950s, with British industry working at full stretch to produce the consumer goods people were

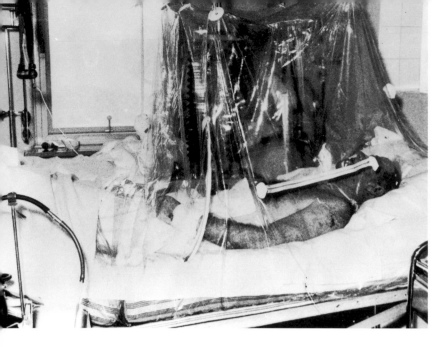

(Left) Matt Busby,
the United manager,
spent many weeks
in an oxygen tent at
the Munich hospital.

now demanding. Cultural change was under-
way, too, notably through the arrival on British
shores of a new kind of music, rock'n'roll, and a
new kind of cinema hero, the young James
Dean. Bill Haley, a somewhat plump individual
with a kiss curl, brought his Comets to Britain
and played 'Rock Around The Clock' in halls up
and down the country earning condemnation
from moral guardians and adulation from
teenagers. Haley would soon look tame beside
Elvis Presley who was to influence millions of
British teenagers in everything from hairstyle to
speech mannerisms. There were even some
home-grown teen idols in the shape of Tommy
Steele and, later, Cliff Richard.

So there was a certain logic to precocious
youth at last having its day, on the football field
as everywhere else. However, in some ways
football lagged behind the rest of the youth
culture. Whereas the new cinema and music
heroes were smouldering young men whom
not many girls would bring home to meet
mother, young footballers of the time had the
appearance of being made in their fathers'
image, suited and short-haired, modest and
polite (at least in public). Part of the
explanation for this dichotomy probably lay in
the fact that whereas stars of rock and movies
were earning fortunes, the Busby Babes and
their ilk were still working under slave labour
conditions. The maximum wage (of £20 a

week) was not abolished until
1961, three years after the Munich
crash. A millennial Duncan Edwards
is guaranteed a fortune. The real
Duncan Edwards never had the
financial rewards that his ability warranted.

United's youngsters may not have been
paid a fortune but they were certainly
celebrities by the mid-1950s. United were
League Champions in the 1955-56 season and
the following year they would go
for an unprecedented treble: the
League, the FA Cup and the
European Cup. This last was a new
competition, invented by the French
sports newspaper *L'Equipe*, and the
English football authorities wanted
nothing to do with it. The previous
season, Chelsea, who had received
an invitation to play in Europe, had
approached the Football League
for permission to enter the
competition. The League
management committee met and
advised Chelsea, in the strongest
terms, to stay out of the European
Cup: there were enough fixtures
already and playing in Europe could
only damage the domestic game.
This was the kind of insularity that
had kept England out of the World
Cup in its early years. It was an
attitude Busby secretly despised. He
was convinced that the British game
could only grow and improve by
exposing itself to European

(Below) Thousands of mourners gathered outside Flixton parish church, near Manchester, for the funeral of United's captain, Roger Byrne.

competition. Continental sides were growing in stature and England had received a fright in 1953 when Hungary, the 'magnificent Magyars', came to Wembley and won 6-3, the first time England had been beaten there. The following year, in Budapest, Hungary beat England 7-1. The writing was on the wall but Busby and Stan Cullis, his opposite number at Wolverhampton Wanderers, seemed to be among the few who could read it.

That first bid for the treble ended with United again winning the League title, reaching the final of the FA Cup and the semi-final of the European Cup. Busby had shown what his youngsters could do as early as the first round of the European Cup that year when, after beating Anderlecht 2-0 in Belgium, United won the second leg 10-0 at Maine Road (Old Trafford had now been rebuilt, but was still without floodlights). United eventually went out

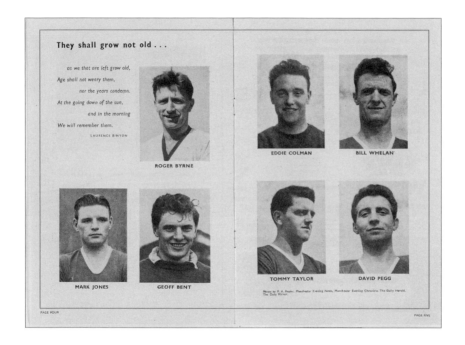

They shall grow not old . . .

as we that are left grow old,
Age shall not weary them,
nor the years condemn.
At the going down of the sun,
and in the morning
We will remember them.

LAURENCE BINYON

ROGER BYRNE

EDDIE COLMAN

BILL WHELAN

MARK JONES

GEOFF BENT

TOMMY TAYLOR

DAVID PEGG

Photos by P. A. Reuter, Manchester Evening News, Manchester Evening Chronicle, The Daily Herald, The Daily Mirror.

PAGE FOUR

PAGE FIVE

end of a first half in which they played football of breathtaking quality. Bobby Charlton had scored two of the goals in the space of three minutes. United had to fight a rearguard action in the second half following injuries to Edwards and Ken Morgan and the match was drawn: enough to take United through. 'As great a performance as I have ever seen from our lads,' Busby said after the match. United, obliged by the English football authorities to play a League match against Wolves three days later (subsequently postponed because of the crash), had little time to celebrate before starting the journey home. It was to be the last journey this team would make together.

Jimmy Murphy did not travel to Belgrade. As well as being Busby's number two, Murphy also managed the Welsh national side, which had an important game that same night, a World Cup qualifier in Cardiff against Israel. Murphy wanted to be in Belgrade but Busby insisted he stay behind and look after Wales. It was a fortuitous decision, for Murphy was be the saving of Manchester United in the weeks and months after the crash. It happened while Murphy was

to Real Madrid, then at the height of their powers, 5-3 on aggregate. But it was clear that Busby's team could compete at the highest European level, even if most people in the corridors of power remained unconvinced and even hostile to United's European adventures. This attitude looks especially odd with the millennium bringing a vast increase in the number of matches that clubs will have to play (and the amount of money they will earn) in European competition, encouraged by their domestic masters at the Football Association and the Premier League.

The following, fateful, year United were optimistic that this time they could go one better and reach the final of the European Cup. United beat Red Star 2-1 in the first leg of the quarter-final. In Belgrade they led 3-0 at the

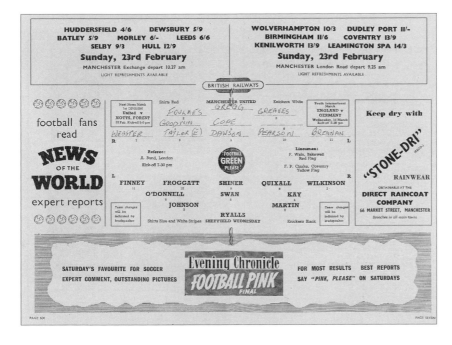

against Sheffield Wednesday the weekend following the crash, it had to be played at some point. Murphy needed players. He signed some from various clubs and at least two rival managers offered to lend him players for nothing. The FA lifted the rule that prevented players playing in the FA Cup for two different sides in the same season. In some respects the game against Sheffield Wednesday at Maine Road, 13 days after the Munich crash, was as unfair to the visitors as it was to United, for there could be only one winner on such a charged occasion: United won 3-0. The programme for the game had a poignancy all its own, for where the names of the United team should have appeared there were eleven blank spaces. Bill Foulkes and Harry Gregg, the goalkeeper, were the only two Munich survivors who played. The victory put United into the sixth round of the Cup where they beat West Bromwich Albion in a replay, by now with Bobby Charlton recovered from the crash and back in the team. Charlton scored in a thrilling semi-final victory, 5-3 against Fulham, and United, a dozen weeks after the worst moment in their history, were in another FA

on a train from Cardiff to Manchester. In *The Team That Wouldn't Die*, John Roberts's definitive account of the Munich disaster, Murphy recalls getting off the train and taking a taxi to Old Trafford. The ground seemed quieter than usual. Murphy poured himself a glass of Scotch. Then Busby's secretary told him about the crash, but Murphy did not take in the full import. In fact, the secretary, Alma George, had to tell Murphy about the crash three times before he took it in: 'A good few minutes had elapsed and suddenly Alma's words began to take effect on me. I went into my office and cried.' Murphy flew to Munich with some of the relatives the following day. Busby was in an oxygen tent. 'Keep the flag flying,' he told Murphy.

Although the Football Association agreed to delay the playing of a fifth round FA Cup tie

Cup final. But the fairytale was not to have the ending that most of the country wanted; Bolton Wanderers beat United at Wembley. But at least Busby, now recovering from the terrible injuries he received at Munich, made the trip to London to watch the match. Five days later, United beat AC Milan 2-1 in the first leg of their European Cup semi-final, but lost 4-0 in Milan in the second leg to go out of the competition.

That match, the last of a long and tragic season, brought down the curtain on the era of the Busby Babes. But what had still to be explained was what caused the crash in which they died. There were four inquiries, two British and two German. The first one, in West Germany (as it then was), decided that the crash was caused by ice on the aircraft's wings. This meant that the crash was effectively Captain Thain's fault; he was the senior pilot and the state of the wings is the responsibility of the aircraft's crew. The next inquiry, in Britain more than two years after the crash, also decided that ice on the wings had been the cause. However, Captain Thain remained convinced the cause of the crash was not ice on the wings but slush on the runway, which would have been the responsibility of Munich airport officials. Thain cited an experiment in America, which had shown that the presence of slush could put enough drag on a plane's progress to slow it down.

The American evidence brought about another German inquiry, but this one reached the same conclusion as the first. There was one thing to give Thain hope: when the second

German report was published in Britain, a report by the Royal Aeronautical Establishment, contradicting the German findings, was published simultaneously. This in turn led to yet another British inquiry, although it involved the same commission as the first one. Even now the definitive cause of the crash had not been established, but at least Thain had won a major victory: in June of 1969, 11 years and three months after the crash, a statement was read in the House of Commons clearing him of any blame. But Thain, who had been dismissed by British European Airways a few months after the crash for allowing his co-pilot to sit in the left-hand seat on the flight back from Belgrade, had not flown since the crash. By the time of the Commons statement his flying licence had expired. Clearly Thain was another victim of the Munich disaster.

As for Manchester United, there were those who said that their like would not be seen again. There were people who thought that Munich could be the start of a long decline in the fortunes of the club. In fact, relative decline was not to come until two decades later, during the 1970s, when United were relegated to the Second Division (now the First) for the first time in their history. A former Old Trafford idol, Denis Law, who had moved to Manchester

City, scored the goal that sent them down. But before the failures of the 1970s, there was a remarkable renaissance, with Busby and Murphy building another great team, one that, at last, would win the European Cup in 1968, making United the first English team to win that trophy (Glasgow Celtic had won it the year before). By then the flowing locks of George Best had replaced the short back and sides haircuts that marked out the 1958 team.

If the team graced by Best, Law, Charlton and the rest never quite acquired the allure of the 1958 side, it was not entirely because of the tragic circumstances of Munich in themselves. The attraction of the Busby Babes was in their very nickname, for if players so young could perform as well as they did, what triumphs might the future hold? It was this, the snatching away of potential, that gave Munich such a resonance, even in the hearts and minds of people far removed from football. More than 40 years after the event, a conversational reference to 'the Munich air crash' rarely needs further amplification.

The Assassination of President Kennedy 1963

THE FERRY BETWEEN PLYMOUTH
and Torpoint is a clanking, shuddering platform
pulled back and forth between the Devon and
Cornish sides of the River Tamar by huge
chains. Late in the afternoon of 22 November
1963, I was a foot passenger on that ferry, an
18-year-old with ambitions to be a journalist
heading for the Torpoint home of a man who
already was one. He was teaching me shorthand. It was an uphill task: Pitman's squiggles
and whirls were impenetrable to me then and
have remained little short of a mystery ever
since. But on that night I at least discovered
that my journalistic instincts, if raw, were all
present and correct.

In the living room of my tutor's home we
sat at a table. A black and white television set,
on but with the sound turned down, stood in
one corner. We noticed some unusual looking
news footage of limousines, running people, a
general air of chaos. My tutor, implored by me,
turned up the sound. 'President John F Kennedy,
travelling through downtown Dallas in an open-
topped car, has been shot.' My tutor switched
off the set: 'We've got more important things
to do', he said. Perhaps he was right, but I
thought he was wrong. I could not get this
shorthand lesson over fast enough. I remember
running back to the ferry, then willing the beast
to set a record for the Tamar crossing. All the
car drivers on the ferry were out of their
vehicles, talking about the news from Dallas,
more than 6000 miles away. By now, shortly
after 7 p.m. in Britain, Kennedy had been
declared dead. Radios all over the ferry carried

There was only one
subject on the minds
of these New York
commuters, following
the shooting in Dallas.

'Camelot era' ends as President Kennedy is gunned down in Dallas

newsflash on the BBC Home Service began: 'News has just come in that President Kennedy has been shot. There's no news yet of his condition.'

Radio Newsreel, the network's flagship evening news programme, interrupted a long feature about the naming of the architect for the new National Theatre in London to carry a live report from Leonard Parkin, the BBC's Washington correspondent, giving more details: 'Mrs Kennedy jumped up and grabbed her husband and cried, "Oh no" as the motorcade sped on. From then on, all was confusion. The police fanned out over a wide area. People screamed and lay down on the ground as the shots were heard. An Associated Press reporter said he saw blood on the President's head. There was absolute pandemonium

around the scene. The secret servicemen who always accompany the President waved the motorcade on at top speed to the hospital but even at high speed it took nearly five minutes to get the car to the ambulance entrance there. For the moment I return you to *Radio Newsreel* in London.'

Minutes later, the sombre tones of the announcer in London delivered the news that all of us listening had feared: 'This is the BBC Home Service. It is with deep regret that we announce that President Kennedy is dead. Mrs Kennedy was in the car with him. The President is reported to have collapsed into her arms, blood pouring from a head wound. He was taken to hospital and given blood transfusions. Two Roman Catholic priests were called, then, half an hour after the shooting, it was

President Kennedy slumps forward and sideways after the shooting and a secret service agent climbs into the car.

announced that the President was dead.' The beginning of that bulletin is interesting, for it reflects a BBC habit of the time: to announce grave news in a way that tends, in Tom Wolfe's much-later phrase about the American tabloid press, 'to identify the correct emotion'. The words, 'it is with deep regret' prepares the listener to respond in a certain way to news that he or she has not yet even heard. There is the ring of a pronouncement from Buckingham Palace rather than a news story. This approach is a characteristic of BBC bulletins going right back to the beginnings in 1922.

News of the assassination spread like a bush fire and was conveyed to people in some strange ways. The President had been declared dead at 1 p.m. Dallas time, 2 p.m. in New York, and 7 p.m. in Britain. Later surveys indicated that, within two hours, 92 per cent of American people knew about the shooting. At a lunchtime concert in Boston, the heartland of the Kennedy clan, the conductor of the Boston Symphony Orchestra told the audience: 'We have a press report over the wires that the President of the United States has been the victim of an assassination. We will play the Funeral March from Beethoven's third symphony.'

Whichever way you announced it and wherever you heard it, the assassination of Kennedy was a fantastic event in a fantastic decade. A generation grew up abruptly when Lee Harvey Oswald unleashed his rifle bullets from a window ledge in the Texas School Book Depository. The Kennedy era has been described by its many chroniclers as 'Camelot'. In that case, Camelot was over. A young President, 43 when he won election in 1960, 46 when he fell to the assassin, had seemed to define and embody an era of new hope, new ideas, new ways forward. Much of this perception was based on rhetoric, but how things seem can be as important in setting a mood as how things actually are. That lesson, well learned by Bill Clinton in America and Tony Blair in Britain, was one for the political textbooks. Put one way, Kennedy was a middle-aged man from a super-rich, privileged background in Massachusetts who won the Presidency against Richard Nixon by the narrowest of margins amid vote-rigging allegations that persist to this day. Put another way, Kennedy was a youthful, fresh-faced war hero who swept into the White House, a beautiful wife on his arm, to inspire millions with his vision of a better America and a better world. A remark typical of the Kennedy style had come ringingly from radio sets in Britain as well as America during Kennedy's inaugural address on 20 January 1961: 'Ask not what your country can do for you, ask what you can do for your country.'

The world was still trying to comprehend what had occurred in Dallas when the beautiful

(Below) Jacqueline
Kennedy, in a suit still
spattered with the
President's blood,
stands beside Lyndon
Johnson as he takes the
Presidential oath
aboard Airforce One.

(Right) The family
after the requiem
mass: Jacqueline with
the late President's
brothers Edward (on
her right), Robert and
the Kennedy children
Carol and John Jr.

wife in question, Jacqueline Kennedy, was shown, pale and distressed but demonstrating enormous dignity, aboard the Presidential aircraft, flying back to Andrew's Air Force base near Washington. She was still in the elegant suit that she was wearing when she cradled her stricken husband's head against her shoulder. The suit was stained with blood. Mrs Kennedy was standing beside Lyndon Johnson, the Vice-President, now swearing the oath of office as he took over the Presidency: the king is dead, long live the king. If the principal drama had already been played out, if the leading character was dead, sub-plots and subsidiary dramas were still to reveal themselves. Oswald was arrested for the killing, only to be shot dead by Jack Ruby, a Dallas night-club owner, while

Oswald was under police escort. Ruby somehow emerged from a scrum of reporters, cameramen, police, FBI agents and assorted bystanders to shoot Oswald at point blank range. Thus did a tragedy take on the elements of a farce. Or was it a conspiracy? From Mark Lane's contemporaneous book, *Rush to Judgment*, to Oliver Stone's movie, *JFK*, thirty years later, the debate about whether Oswald was the lone assassin, whether Ruby was paid by dark forces to ensure that an inconvenient trial would never take place, has raged down the years. The death of John Fitzgerald Kennedy gave life to an industry.

Long before Dallas, there had been no shortage of drama surrounding the Kennedy presidency. Few people outside the ranks of political junkies (and I admit my own addiction) recall much about Kennedy's domestic policies, because the memory of his time in office is dominated by three events that were bound up with the former Soviet Union, plus his fateful decision to involve America in the Vietnam War. The least of these events, Kennedy's visit to Berlin to reassure the people of what was then West Germany about their security, is recalled as the setting for one of Kennedy's most famous soundbites: 'Ich bin ein Berliner'. The statement survives in the archive of great moments from the Cold War, even though it literally translates,

to Berliners, as 'I am a donut'. Never mind, Berlin cheered Kennedy to the echo.

Attitudes to the Bay of Pigs fiasco of 1961 and the Cuban missile crisis the following year are less easy to encapsulate. The Bay of Pigs was Kennedy's first foreign adventure in office and his first disaster, although mitigation is necessary here. Ever since the fall of Batista and the arrival in power of Fidel Castro in 1959 there had been a kind of panic in the US which was never properly understood in Europe. But then, Europe is not 90 miles from Cuba. Florida is. The Bay of Pigs plan, under which American marines would go ashore in Cuba and link up with anti-Castro elements to overthrow the revolutionary president, had been conceived by the Central Intelligence Agency and given the nod by the previous administration. The plan had a madly optimistic look to it and so it proved; the 'invasion' was an embarrassing

failure and America was made to look silly. The calamity angered Kennedy, but before long there came a test that was to push the Bay of Pigs into the margins of history. Cuba would once more be centre stage, but this time the world was to stare into the nuclear abyss.

Kennedy was a Democrat but he was no soft touch where the Communists were concerned. He committed ever-increasing numbers of troops to Vietnam as a way of demonstrating his anti-Communist credentials. The adventure in faraway south-east Asia was to haunt Kennedy and two of his successors, Johnson and Nixon, all three of them blighted by a war the American people did not want and the American nation could not win. The cost was to be half a million US casualties terminating in ignominious withdrawal 25 years after Kennedy came to office. But his words in that 1961 inaugural address should have prepared America and the world for the Kennedy approach to foreign aggressors. They would not, he made clear, find Jack Kennedy lacking resolve:

'Let every nation know, whether it wishes us well or ill, that we shall pay any price, bear any burden, meet any hardship, support any friend, oppose any foe to assure the success and survival of liberty.'

If Nikita Khrushchev, the Soviet leader, was listening to that in Moscow, he seems to have decided to test Kennedy sooner rather than later. American U-2 spy planes had already identified sites in Cuba, which were being prepared, said the intelligence analysts, to receive missiles. This news infuriated the American people and added to the volatility of the US-Soviet relationship. The Soviets had already put the *Sputnik* in orbit, beating America into space and inducing a frenzy in the American press, which painted a picture of Soviet missiles being hurled at America from the skies like stones from a motorway bridge. Kennedy pledged that America would put a

man on the moon by the end of the 1960s, a pledge fulfilled in 1969, six years after Dallas. There was something about the gentle bleep-bleep emitted by *Sputnik* that seemed to be mocking America, a nation that assumed itself to be the leader in all things technical. It was as if a baseball team from Vladivostok had beaten the Boston Red Sox.

Threats and counter-threats relating to the Cuban sites had been passing back and forth for some time but the kettle really started boiling in the seven days leading up to Sunday 28 October. It is not overstating the matter to say that there were many millions of rational people, in the US and Britain and other countries, who felt that the Cold War was about to turn hot. To young people at the end of the century, this must sound an absurd and irrational reaction. After all, the Soviet empire has gone now and its core country, Russia, is an economic basket case. Much of the Russian submarine fleet, feared as the agent of death by two generations of Westerners, now sits idle in dock, its unpaid officers living aboard with their families. Washing lines are attached to the conning towers.

The very element that contributed to the collapse of Russia, the arms race, was what made us fearful in 1962 that a nuclear holocaust was about to be unleashed. The arms race was at full throttle when Kennedy stood toe to toe with Khrushchev. By the beginning of that last full week in October, the clock was running and its ticking was beginning to sound ominously like that of a bomb. Britain was very much involved. One reporter, working for a

Glasgow newspaper, had been sent up to the Holy Loch, where Britain's *Polaris* nuclear submarine fleet was based, to see if there was any activity. There was none, which was in itself frightening. The entire *Polaris* fleet appeared to have gone to sea. At Holy Loch, there was no sign of life.

Meanwhile Soviet cargo ships steamed towards Cuba. American reconnaissance aircraft photographed them and the published results clearly showed what looked like the outline of missiles on the ships' decks, covered with tarpaulins. Kennedy told Khrushchev to turn the ships around. Khrushchev refused. In downtown America, people were installing nuclear shelters. In London, some of the members of a group of Campaign for Nuclear Disarmament protesters, who had been camped outside the American embassy, left for a remote part of western Ireland, believing that all-out nuclear war was imminent. They were by no means the only ones, but on Sunday 28 October the crisis suddenly ended. It ended with a radio announcement. Khrushchev had arranged to make a statement on Moscow Radio but until it was broadcast the West had no way of knowing what he would say. Khrushchev announced that missiles already in Cuba would be dismantled and taken back to the Soviet Union. Ships *en route* to Cuba that were carrying missiles would turn back. The demand that the US remove Nato missiles from Turkey, with which the Soviet Union had a border, was

dropped. In return, Kennedy announced the end of the Cuban blockade and gave a promise that the island would not be invaded.

The world breathed again. But the crisis had brought a distinct, if subtle, change in attitudes, especially among young people. The Cold War had always threatened instant oblivion, now there was evidence that politicians were willing to deliver it. Kennedy had called the Soviet bluff, but what if it had not been called? What if there was to be a next time? No poker player wins every night. There was a sense that if the present had been secured, the future was even more uncertain than it had looked before the US and the Soviet Union locked horns. The 1960s fashion for Jean. Paul Sartre's existentialism now took on a deeper resonance. Living for now not only seemed convenient, it seemed positively wise. This attitudinal change was to impact on the decade as a whole, manifesting itself in the student demonstrations in Paris, London, Washington and elsewhere. The drugs culture also drew on the missile crisis for its somewhat bogus rationale: if danger was to rain down from the skies at any moment, why not at least court the sort of danger one might fleetingly enjoy? The argument sounded a lot more convincing through a haze of cannabis smoke than it ever could in the cold light of reasoned argument, nonetheless it had its proponents in every corner of the modern culture, from academia to the pop charts.

If the missile crisis helped that attitude take hold, the killing of Kennedy in some senses gave it further credence. The great hope of the

President Kennedy chairs a cabinet meeting during the missile crisis.

young had been snatched away in a rattle of gunfire, so clearly (the argument went) there was little point in placing your hope in political jousting, which suddenly looked a less edifying spectacle now that the glamorous man on the white charger had been removed from the ring. In the assassination's aftermath, the world listened and watched as the old guard returned to the foreground. For the fresh-faced Kennedy, read Johnson, a man with a huge head and a face like a contour map, who had about him the look of an old-style pragmatist. Gone were Kennedy's cultured, rounded New England vowels, replaced by the Texan drawl of Johnson, whose crudity of expression and pragmatism of outlook were both summed up in a remark attributed to him when someone suggested that he get rid of J Edgar Hoover, the legendary chief of the FBI. Johnson said: 'I'd rather have Hoover inside the tent pissing out than outside the tent pissing in'. It was not easy to imagine that kind of talk in the Kennedy White House, at least not on the evidence available at the time. Even the name of the new First Lady seemed to say something about the change that was taking place: the elegantly named Jacqueline was now replaced by someone called Lady Bird.

Of course, the fact that Johnson would do more for civil rights and welfare reform than Kennedy ever managed was overlooked by those who saw the end of Camelot as the death of hope. It was not, but it seemed as if it was. And it certainly ended what looks at this distance like an age of innocence for the American political establishment. When Kennedy came to the White House, its sloping front lawn was open to Pennsylvania Avenue and office girls would lounge on the grass every lunchtime, eating their sandwiches. Soon after Dallas, black railings were installed to cut off the building from the public. They are still there, a permanent reminder of democracy's vulnerability to anarchy. In other, more prosaic matters, a shocked world continued to function. British television viewers had spent the night of 22 November watching the bloody termination of the life of a real hero, an event that unfolded in real time. The next night, they sat down to watch a fictional hero who could live in any time he chose: on 23 November, BBC television showed the very first episode of *Doctor Who*.

England Win the World Cup 1966

Britain's dominance of the Swinging Sixties sealed on Wembley's turf

Bobby Moore is borne aloft by Geoff Hurst (left) and Ray Wilson after receiving the trophy from The Queen.

THEY COULD NOT HAVE EXPLAINED the offside rule to save their lives. They would rather spend Saturday afternoon in a supermarket or a science park than a football stadium. Yet on Sunday 31 July 1966, millions of people in England woke up having acquired the curious ability to recite 11 names: Banks, Cohen, Wilson, Stiles, Charlton J, Moore, Ball, Hunt, Charlton R, Hurst and Peters. They also knew that these men, heroes all, had their own hero in a middle-aged man called Alf Ramsey, who sounded as if he had enrolled for a course of elocution lessons (he had) but left the class halfway through (he had not). England, for the first time, had won the football World Cup at Wembley on Saturday 30 July and in doing so they had put the icing on the cake of a delicious, mad, disastrous, triumphant and, yes, very British, decade.

The importance of what was to happen at Wembley could be measured on the streets of England, if not of Britain (in Scotland, certainly, people determinedly went about other business, or claimed to be doing so). English streets were all but empty. Buses travelled their usual routes, but the driver was also the only passenger. Shops either installed television sets or closed down for the duration. Patrolling police officers somehow found their attention drawn to the windows of shops that sold televisions, shops which became, for two hours, the most guarded in the country. Outside Wembley, before the final against West Germany, there was an atmosphere of VE Day, a comparison that was persistently made without anyone quite drawing explicit attention to the fact that England's opponents that day came from the country that had been defeated 21 years earlier. This, after all, was only a football match. Of course it was.

The television audience, worldwide, was 400 million, their pictures delivered by the BBC. They saw a final that was not as great as it is sometimes painted, though it was certainly dramatic. Germany went ahead, England equalized, England went ahead, Germany equalized seconds from the end of normal time. Then, in the extra half hour, two more goals from England, the first hotly disputed but awarded after a lengthy conversation between a referee from Switzerland and a linesman from Azerbaijan. The final score: 4-2. The last goal was

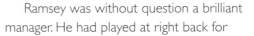

accompanied, for television viewers, by what is perhaps the most famous piece of commentary in sporting history. The BBC commentator, Kenneth Wolstenholme, saw Geoff Hurst collect the ball inside the German half but noticed, out of the corner of an eye, that a few English fans were approaching the pitch, anticipating the final whistle. Hurst strode forward with the ball, into the left side of the German penalty area. 'Some people are on the pitch,' Wolstenholme said, 'they think it's all over…' Hurst ignored little Alan Ball, who was galloping into the penalty area and screaming for a pass, and instead lashed a glorious, rising shot past Tilkowski, the German goalkeeper; '…it is now' Wolstenholme said.

A fairy-tale. The country that invented football had at last contrived to win the World Cup, which had been played every four years, outside of wartime, since 1930. When the 16 finalists assembled for the tournament the outcome could hardly have been less predictable. Home advantage was known to be a considerable factor, it had been shown in previous World Cups, but few people actually thought that England would win the tournament. Ramsey had been in charge for three years and he was one of the few; in an interview shortly after becoming manager, he implied that he thought England would win in 1966. For a man so cautious in his public statements, this was a spectacular prediction. He probably thought himself lucky when most people forgot it.

Ramsey was without question a brilliant manager. He had played at right back for Tottenham and England and even in his playing days he would spend hours talking to coaches about tactics. His management chance came at Ipswich Town, then languishing in the game's lower reaches. He took them from the bottom division to the top in six years, including promotion from the Second Division and the championship of the First (now the Premier League) in successive seasons. But could he make world champions of England? They had not done much in World Cups thus far and the domestic game was not in very good order, attendances having slumped dramatically since the

post-war boom. English football desperately needed a successful World Cup.

The tournament started with an unpromising 0-0 draw against Uruguay but wins over France and Mexico, each by 2-0, left England as winners of their group. From then on, the World Cup would be on a knockout basis: one defeat and you were out. The quarter-final was a vicious encounter with Argentina, during which the Argentine captain, Rattin, was sent off for arguing. At first Rattin refused to go. The crowd went berserk. Eventually Rattin, head hung down, two fingers raised to the baying English fans, trudged towards the touchline. Tackles were coming in like scythes in a hayfield. The great Jimmy Greaves had been left out because of a gashed leg, but he had not sparked in the tournament

and Ramsey was ready to drop him anyway. In came Hurst for his first game of the World Cup. And, in the second half, Hurst scored, a header from a looping cross by his clubmate at West Ham, Martin Peters. 1-0. Game over.

The semi-final, against Portugal, was three days later, on Tuesday 26 July. By this time the nation had given up pretending to be indifferent to football. The pound sterling may have been going down the Swanee, anti-Vietnam protesters may have been tearing up Grosvenor Square, Mao Tse-Tung may have been about to announce his Cultural Revolution… Who cared? The only question anyone in England was interested in was whether Alf – we were all on familiar terms with him by now – would bring back Greaves or stick with Hurst. The answer was that he would stick with Hurst. But on this occasion, there was a match within a match: Stiles, the toothless terrier with the number four on his back, versus Eusebio, the elegant, brilliant, Portuguese man-o'-goals, a player so good that, like Pele or God, he appeared to need only the one name.

Amazingly, Stiles won the match within a match and so England won the game. It was, by common consent, the game of the tournament so far. Ramsey had confounded the pundits by not asking Stiles to man mark Eusebio, though it was usually Stiles who was there whenever Eusebio turned around. Stiles was a great marker, he could separate a man from his shadow, and he had a great match. So did Bobby Charlton, who scored both goals in a 2-1 win. But football had a great match, too. The game itself was graced by the way those 22 men played it, typified by what happened when Charlton ran back after the thunderous shot that was his second goal. A succession of Portuguese players held out their hands to congratulate him. At the end of the game, back in the dressing room, the England players gave Stiles a round of applause. Across the corridor, Eusebio, who had scored Portugal's goal from the penalty spot, was in tears.

That was a better game than the final, though not of course anything like as dramatic. But the importance of England winning the World Cup could not be over-stated. Harold Wilson, British Prime Minister of the time, had fought an election in April, having led a minority government since 1964, and secured a 96-seat majority, which he subsequently attributed, in

part, to the euphoria that was building ahead of the World Cup. But the tournament arrived at a time of chaos in the British economy and turmoil in the political circles charged with doing something about it. The government imposed a prices and incomes freeze which infuriated the trade unions; there was to be a devaluation of the pound sterling in 1967. On the international stage, Wilson was locked in a battle with the truculent Prime Minister of Rhodesia, Ian Smith, who had made a unilateral declaration of independence from the British colonial power.

None of which overshadowed the real achievement of the 1960s, which was that it went into history as the most socially exciting of the century.

The victory at Wembley was only one of the signals that Britain had at last shaken off its image as a dour country, still carting the baggage of its imperial past and still trying to recover from the ravages of World War II.

FORTY CENTS

APRIL 15, 1966

LONDON: The Swinging City

TIME

THE WEEKLY NEWSMAGAZINE

VOL. 87 NO. 15

The world had gazed into the nuclear abyss during the Cuban missile crisis of 1962 and, perhaps because of that, perhaps in spite of it, young people were beginning to forget the long term and start enjoying the benefits of the social and technological change that was all around them. These changes were going on everywhere in the Western world, but Britain was a microcosm for all of them. In April of 1966, *Time* magazine ran a cover story – 'London: The Swinging City' – which put the term 'swinging London' into the lexicon of modern life. It declared: 'In a decade dominated by youth, London has burst into bloom. It swings, it is the scene.'

In art, theatre, cinema, fashion and music many of the main movers and shakers were now to be found in London. But medicine and politics were to play an equal part in changing the face of Britain. The 1960s saw the arrival of the birth pill, which heralded a sexual revolution. Young women were no longer at the mercy of their bodies, or their men, in matters of birth control. In 1967, the British House of Commons legalized abortion and that, plus the decriminalization of homosexuality, transformed the moral landscape. Drugs also became a major factor for the first time. But the commonly heard remark about the decade, that if you could remember it you weren't there, overstated the role of cannabis and other drugs. Rock stars may have been smoking, sniffing and injecting at a rate that would do none of them much good (and did some of them fatal harm), but the wider population remained touchingly loyal to the traditional outlets, booze and tobacco.

The decade began and ended with achievements in space. In 1961 the Soviet Union startled the world by announcing that their cosmonaut, Yuri Gagarin, had become the first man in space, and in 1969 the Americans put Neil Armstrong on the moon. These huge technological achievements contributed to a feeling that mankind had

(Below) Martin Luther
King delivering his
'I have a dream' speech
at the Lincoln Memorial
in Washington DC.

(Right) The uprising
by French students
was short-lived but
included some ugly
scenes, including this
attack by riot police
in Paris.

conquered his environment and was now
ready to take on the universe.

This was a simplistic notion, for between
Gagarin circling the Earth ('the sky looks very
very dark and the Earth bluish') and Armstrong
setting foot on the moon ('one small step for
man, one giant leap for mankind') there was
enough excitement, turmoil, triumph and
tragedy back on our own planet to keep
social commentators busy for years.

Britain's speciality seemed to be spies, cars
and pop singers. From the arrest of Gordon
Lonsdale in 1961 to the escape from jail of
George Blake in 1966, spy scandals were a
dominant feature of the decade. So were cars,
from the launching of that 1960s icon, the
E-type Jaguar, in 1961 to the continuing saga of
the distressed volume car industry, lurching

from financial crisis to strike to financial crisis to
another strike. But it was pop singers who
really put British mass culture on the map with
the emergence in 1961 of The Beatles, a
Liverpool group with haircuts resembling
upturned mops. John Lennon, Paul McCartney,
George Harrison and Ringo Starr had been
brought up in Liverpool, a once-great port
city fallen on harder times. The group had
plenty of rivals, including a southern contender
in the Rolling Stones from London, but
somehow The Beatles rose to the top of the
pile and stayed there.

Lennon and McCartney were the driving
forces. They wrote all the music, which was
heavily influenced by American rhythm and
blues records that the pair had bought from
seamen arriving at Liverpool docks. The group
found a new sound and the
public lapped it up, giving The
Beatles a string of number one
hits. Their story was in some
ways the story of youth in that
decade, moving from longish but
neat haircuts above smart suits,
all the way to the beards and
robes garb that characterized
the later 1960s, influenced as it
was by the Indian mystics that
the group took to visiting on
remote mountain tops. Such
places were a far cry from
Penny Lane and the Cavern
Club in Liverpool and you
sensed that the sceptical
Lennon, for one, never really

thought that a maharishi might have the answer to all his problems.

There was other important music being generated in the 1960s and some of it was much less mainstream than that of The Beatles, who for all their cheeky remarks and rebellious appearance were pretty much a commercial band designed to sell records. Across the Atlantic, a newspaper report in September 1961 had said: 'A surprising young talent with a frayed appearance and compelling stage presence is generating the kind of excitement in New York's Greenwich Village normally reserved for grizzled veterans of the folk music scene'. This was Bob Dylan, a small 20-year-old with a guitar who soon became the most celebrated folk singer, especially for his protest songs, since Woody Guthrie. There was plenty to protest about, for the youth revolt that was another characteristic of the decade, culminating in student riots in Paris, London and on American campuses, both inspired and was inspired by singers such as Dylan and his contemporary Joan Baez. The American involvement in Vietnam and civil rights for black Americans were the two key issues.

It was July 1964 when President Lyndon Johnson signed into law the most sweeping package of reforms in American social history, giving black people fundamental rights that were taken as read by whites. There had been bloody battles for reform, especially in the American South, where until the new laws black people could not sit in the same part of a bus as whites and had to attend different schools. Blacks and whites could not even use the same drinking fountains. So the reforms were long overdue and Johnson, himself a Southerner who was deeply conscious of the redneck attitudes still prevalent in his own state, Texas, went on television and radio to say: 'Let us close the springs of racial poison'. The complete end of segregation was several years away and in March 1965 Dr Martin Luther King led one of the biggest anti-racism protests when 25,000 marched to the state government building in Montgomery, Alabama. Not all of the race protests were in the South, nor were they all peaceful: the Los Angeles district of Watts erupted in flames in August 1965 after the arrest of a black man, and paratroopers had to be called in to quell a riot in Detroit in July 1967.

Vietnam would remain on the agenda for another 10 years or more, but the escalation of the war in the 1960s brought protest marches on Washington, the burning of draft cards and the jailing of young men who refused to go. The most famous 'draft dodger' was the boxer, Cassius Clay, who had become Muhammad Ali and refused the draft on religious grounds. He was not jailed but he was stripped of his world championship and banned from fighting for nearly four years. These were some of the outward signals, serious and frivolous, of a world in transition: from the postwar austerity, in which the old order remained dominant, to a more modern and affluent age, in which younger voices sought to have their say. The point was not that they did, but that they were to grow to become the generation in power. They would bring with them into power some of the values espoused in their youth.

The step from such grand thoughts to a mere football match may seem a large and unlikely one but the fact is that Wembley on that July day in 1966 brought to the centre of the world stage some of the young men who encompassed this new spirit. They were from the first generation of footballers to play after the game had abolished the maximum wage (in 1961), so these were players from a new and affluent working class. Already the Irish star George Best of Manchester United was established as a youth icon at least as potent as The Beatles. But this Wembley occasion was not for him. This was for English and German stars, a World Cup final that could not have been better from the standpoint of

surely take off. It was only in the spring of 1999, during a radio interview, that I heard Stiles explain just what was going on. Stiles, who wore glasses and false teeth off the pitch, was trying to spot his wife in the crowd. He knew she would be wearing a dark blue skirt and a white blouse, for those were England's usual colours. However, West Germany also played in white shirts, so England changed to red. As Stiles waved and danced and shouted, his wife waved back, but he could not see her. Unknown to Stiles, the great German player Uwe Seeler was just behind him and Seeler was delighted to see this attractive young

the organizers even if the draw had been made in football heaven.

Countless images have stayed with those of us who saw the game – and you only had to be alive to be in that category – but there is one that I put above all the others. Nobby Stiles, the combative little midfield player, danced around the pitch at the end, after the ceremonials, pumping his legs and waving his arms as if possessed. At one point Stiles seemed to be waving so hard that he would

woman, dressed in the German colours, waving at him. Seeler waved back. Stiles kept waving, his wife kept waving, Seeler kept waving. In the middle of a cacophonous celebration, the crowning moment in the entire history of English football, a player from each side and one of their wives were engaged in a bizarre ritual, without any of them quite understanding what was going on. Somehow the moment summed up not so much the match, more the entire decade. But you had to be there.

Men on the Moon 1969

One small step – America triumphant as first men walk on the moon

Buzz Aldrin faces the Stars and Stripes, which later blew over when the astronauts lifted off *en route* for home.

THE USUAL SUNDAY MORNING casual drift out of sleep into wakefulness did not apply on 20 July 1969. The world was up and about and was to spend the day tracking the progress of a tiny craft on a mission far from Earth. By the time the craft reached its target, most of us, hundreds of millions of us, were tuned in to the radio or ranged in front of the television. It was afternoon in the United States, mid-evening in Britain, midnight in the Middle East, near dawn in Asia. Wherever and whoever we were, we had gazed as children at the yellow oval in the sky, yearning to make its strange dark shadings into the shape of a face so that we, too, could say that we had seen the man in the moon. On that Sunday, this imaginative leap, one of the staples of childhood, was to be made redundant.

Nearly a quarter of a million miles from where we gathered, Neil Armstrong and Buzz Aldrin were standing, in boots and helmets and pressurized spacesuits, gazing through their visors at the ground rushing towards them. What they were looking at was the surface of the moon and they were the first earthlings to see it this close. Their landing craft, called *Eagle*, had detached itself from the mother ship, called *Columbia*, and was now in the inexorable grip of the moon's gravitational field. Armstrong and Aldrin were flying backwards, their eyes glued to an array of instruments which told them their speed, rate of descent, height above the moon's surface, direction and so on. Across the ether from Mission Control in Houston, Texas, came the voice of another astronaut, Charlie Duke: '*Eagle*, Houston. If you read, you're GO

and offices. People in cars pulled off highways to listen. The public address systems in large stores gave up notifying shoppers of half-price butter bargains on aisle number eight and instead started relaying the drama from space. Aldrin and Armstrong kept gazing at their dials. There was a brief scare when an alarm sounded but that turned out to be computer overload: the dread word abort would not be needed. At 4,000 feet (1,200 metres) above the moon, there was a key moment when Mission Control had to give approval (or not) to go ahead with the landing. Hundreds of men, arranged in tiers at Mission Control like a hi-tech grandstand, gazed at screens to check that all was well. It was. Duke spoke: 'Eagle, you're GO for landing'.

The final descent began 1,300 feet (400 metres) above the moon's surface. Now Armstrong and Aldrin could glance through the triangular windows at the surface of the moon. They knew, from the simulations, from the countless photographs taken on unmanned missions, what the landing site was supposed to look like. And this was not it. They had overshot

for powered descent'. Michael Collins, who was in the command module circling in lunar orbit, relayed his words to Eagle: 'Eagle this is Columbia. They just gave you a GO for powered descent.'

Eagle was now entering the final phase of a journey into history. All around the world, the millions listening and watching heard these exchanges relayed from Houston. As the moment grew closer, work stopped in factories

The rocket carrying Apollo 11 to the moon rises from the launchpad.

by four miles. Now Armstrong would have to fly the ship by hand, he would have to look for another landing site, a gap between the huge boulders that were all over the place. Armstrong guided *Eagle*, Aldrin called out the speed, height, all the numbers that were vital to a safe landing. The most vital number of all was the amount of fuel left, which was measured in terms of how long it would take to use it up. 'Ninety seconds', Aldrin called. Mission Control fell silent. They knew that *Eagle* would crash if it ran out of fuel and there was every chance that, if that happened, the first two men on the moon would be stranded there.

Armstrong had found a landing place, an area where the boulders at last gave way to a flat, featureless surface, ideal for landing. How much fuel was left? 'Sixty seconds'. Armstrong aimed the ship for the new landing site. 'Thirty seconds', said Aldrin. *Eagle* was now 50 feet (15 metres) above the moon. Then 30 feet (9 metres). Then… 'Kicking up some dust', said Aldrin. Then… 'Faint shadow', said Aldrin. Then… 'Contact light!', said Aldrin. This meant that the four pads on the legs of *Eagle* were in touch with the ground, but Armstrong had landed so smoothly Aldrin could hardly believe it. Mission Control's computers also suggested that *Eagle* was down, but in Houston nobody was going to believe a computer, not at that stage. They would, however, believe Armstrong. They waited. Nothing. It took some three seconds for the sound of the human voice to travel back and forth between moon and Earth and in these circumstances three seconds was eternity. At last the communication line clicked

open again. It was Armstrong: 'Houston. Tranquility Base here. The *Eagle* has landed.'

The achievement heralded by those words would have been great enough in isolation, but it was made all the greater when set against the years of frustration, and indeed humiliation, which had preceded it. Until the moon landing, the space race between the superpowers, the US and the USSR, was being won hands down by the latter. The Soviet Union had been the first to place a satellite in orbit, first to send an unmanned probe to the moon, first to place a human in space, first to orbit two manned craft at the same time. The scientific challenge had undoubtedly been met, first and best, by the Soviet Union. But America was to catch up, and perhaps overtake, by becoming first to meet the romantic challenge, that of placing men on the moon.

It is impossible to overstate what the landing meant for America's self esteem, its sense of place in the world. The first Soviet spacecraft, called *Sputnik*, had circled the earth in 1957, sending its bleep-bleep signal out for all

to hear. *Sputnik* weighed 184 lbs (83 kg) and
was not much bigger than a basketball. Four
years later, American astronauts in training
for the Mercury programme, which was to
produce the first American in orbit, were
woken up in the middle of the night to
discover that the first American would not be
the first human in orbit. That privilege had gone
to Yuri Gagarin, a handsome young Russian.
Sputnik and Gagarin between them caused a
great panic in the United States, a tremendous
outburst of self-doubt and even self-loathing.
Soviet rockets were sailing into space,
American rockets were routinely (or so it
seemed) blowing up on launchpads or, as
happened on one dreadful occasion, failing
even to ignite. The word 'sputnik' became a
taunt that the American press, often using
black humour, turned against its own space
community. It culminated in a New York
tabloid's headline over a story about one failed
American launch: KAPUTNIK! The American
public and the American media were in full cry.

In reality the Mercury programme was
going reasonably well. Seven pilots had been
chosen to become America's first astronauts
and they were made into national heroes
overnight. The media may not have thought
much of America's rockets but they knew an
American hero when they met one. Indeed, the
apparent unreliability of the Atlas rockets then
being tested made the seven all the more
heroic. The men had done nothing yet but they
were already icons. They signed a deal with *Life*
magazine and they would produce a book, *We
Seven*, about the Mercury programme. Their

wives and children became public possessions.
The seven were: Scott Carpenter, Gordon
Cooper, John Glenn, Gus Grissom, Wally
Schirra, Alan Shepard and Deke Slayton. From
these seven would come America's first man in
space. Even before that happened, the space
programme would get renewed impetus when,
also in 1961, President Kennedy pledged that
America would put a man on the moon before
the decade was over. Cynics claimed this was a
stunt: Kennedy had just emerged from the Bay
of Pigs fiasco with his poll ratings at their lowest
ever. Whatever it was, the National Aeronautics
and Space Administration (NASA) was now
charged with turning a dream into reality.

By the time Shepard became the first
American to make a sub-orbital flight around
the Earth, and John Glenn became the first
American in Earth orbit, America had
recovered much of the lost ground. Not that
the seven astronauts had ever understood
what all the fuss about, for they knew all about
experimental flying and they knew that
experiments sometimes went wrong: that was
the whole point of experiments. The seven,
who emerged from a rigorous testing
programme conducted at Edwards Airforce
Base in California's Mojave Desert – a place
about as hospitable as the surface of the moon
– had no doubt that space flight was just a
matter of getting the technology right. And the
technology was certainly getting there, for
developments in two different fields over the
preceding two decades meant that the key
components in space flight, computers and
rocket fuel, had now reached a point of

evolution which fitted them perfectly for the race into space. Everything was coming together nicely.

However, none of the seven realized that the moon was a realistic target until Shepard went to the White House to collect a medal from President Kennedy. Afterwards, Kennedy took Shepard and a few NASA officials into the Oval Office. Kennedy sat down in a rocking chair. He wanted to know what NASA was going to do, far into the future. Shepard recalls

thinking: 'My God! These guys are thinking about sending a man to the moon.' As if reading his thoughts, Kennedy turned to Shepard: 'We're not about to put you guys on a rocket and send you to the moon,' he said. 'We're just thinking about it.' Less than three weeks later, in a speech to the US Congress, Kennedy made his pledge about putting a man on the moon by the end of the decade. The crowds that turned out for Shepard and the even larger ones when Glenn received a ticker-tape wel-

come in New York after orbiting the Earth had shown Kennedy that America had an appetite bordering on a lust for the space project.

There was a long road ahead, pock-marked with triumphs and disasters and shadowed all the way by the Soviets. But by the latter half of the 1960s Moscow's famed rockets were starting to look more vulnerable, with many of them blowing up on the launch sites. Of course, unlike America's efforts, the Soviet ones did not blow up all over the nation's television screens. And the Soviets kept finding the money for more rockets. Early in 1969, Central Intelligence Agency photographs showed a rocket the size of a 30-storey building standing on a launch site in Russia. It was called N-1 and the photographs, plus other intelligence gathered by the CIA, suggested that the only possible purpose of N-1 was to put a man on the moon. NASA, shown the pictures by the CIA, remained confident that America could get there first, but clearly there was no time to be lost. The Apollo programme, successor to Mercury, was now well under way and the personalities who would soon become national treasures were beginning to loom

larger in the public consciousness. Apollo 8, which had orbited the moon, had a back-up crew consisting of Armstrong, Aldrin and Collins. The form was that the back-up crew on a given flight would form the main crew three flights thereafter, so Armstrong, Aldrin and Collins were called in by Slayton, by now in charge of assigning crews. In his book *Moon Shot*, written jointly with Shepard (though Slayton died before it was finished), Slayton recalls telling the three men: 'You're it, guys. You've got the Apollo 11 flight and that means you get first crack at landing on the moon. That is, of course, if we pull off successful missions with nine and ten.' Both flights had their problems but nothing that was serious enough to stand in the way of a moon landing with Apollo 11.

Thus it was that on that historic 20 July, Armstrong stepped out of the lunar module and climbed down a ladder to the surface of the moon. To those watching on television it seemed to take a long time. Ordinary mortals would probably have missed out the steps and jumped, but Armstrong was a man made of the right stuff. There was no hurry, but there was a jump: it was three feet or more from the bottom step to the surface and Armstrong jumped that. He paused, planting his boots firmly on the ground. He spoke the words that he had worked out long in advance, and upwards of half a billion people around the world heard him:

'That's one small step for man, one giant leap for mankind.' Mission Control whooped, America whooped, most of the world whooped. You could be a cynic about a lot of things, but it was hard to be a cynic about this.

You could wonder whether there was much in the way of a scientific dividend from simply landing on the moon and then flying home again, but this was not the moment for such thoughts. All you could do was watch in awe.

You could also spare a thought for Collins, up there in the command module, 50 miles (80 km) above the moon, going round in circles. So near, so far. But these were men who accepted their role, they had that kind of discipline, so you did not have to feel sorry for Collins for long. Instead, you turned back to the television to watch Aldrin, 15 minutes after Armstrong, come down the steps and take his place in history, 'buoyant and full of goose pimples'. As Armstrong and Aldrin got used to an environment where gravity was one-sixth of

that on Earth, they started to take cautious
steps and soon seemed to be bouncing along.
It was plain that they were starting to enjoy
themselves, in fact Armstrong was to report
that they felt like 'bug-eyed boys in a candy
store'. But NASA was determined to behave
like a stern parent and had allocated the men
only two hours on the moon. They had much
to do and the children analogy now switched
from candy store to beach: the astronauts had
brought buckets and spades, into which they
scooped as many soil samples as possible: from
the fine, powdery stuff to lumps of rock.
Armstrong kept up a running commentary,
introducing to the watching millions various
mundane bits of equipment which suddenly
became exotic. There was a 'collection sample
rod', for example, and a 'contingency sample
collector'. Whatever these were, nobody had
one in their tool shed.

After a couple of hours the astronauts went
back to *Eagle*. They slept, fitfully, for five hours.
Two human beings, asleep on the surface of the
moon. It was fantastic, when you came to think
about it. They woke up, or rather Houston
woke them up. They fired up the engine and
lifted off. The down draught produced a
mini-storm of debris, in which the American

flag that the two men had planted on the
moon got knocked over on its side. The men
had also left a plaque on the moon, giving the
date of the mission and its origin and stating its
purpose as being 'for all mankind'. In 10 minutes
Eagle docked with *Columbia* in a perfect
manoeuvre. Armstrong and Aldrin rejoined
Collins and the three of them let rip a fit of
giggles and shouts and wide-eyed smiles, their
first chance to celebrate together. Then the two
moonwalkers transferred their kit from *Eagle*
to *Columbia* and *Eagle* was cast adrift. It would
orbit the moon for a few weeks before
crashing on its surface.

The trip home would be routine, at least
by the standards now in place. So it proved.
Columbia splashed down, the three astronauts —
no, national heroes — were pulled out and
taken home. America rejoiced, once more
certain that it led the world. The panic, the
national mania, of the late 1950s and early
1960s now gave way to a more balanced, even
complacent, atmosphere. Incredibly, the race
for space that politicians in Moscow and
Washington had thought, a few short years
before, was a race for the very survival of
mankind now resolved itself into nothing less
than a partnership. In July 1975, six years after

Apollo 11, a joint US-USSR operation, involving an Apollo and a Soviet Soyuz spacecraft, would climax successfully 140 miles (225 km) above the Atlantic ocean, where the two craft docked. The commanders, Tom Stafford and Alexei Leonov, shook hands through the hatches of their craft and exchanged greetings, Leonov in English and Stafford in Russian. The significance of the moment was much more than technical, though it had that aspect. Both the Soviets and the Americans had realized that, if one of their spacecraft became stranded in space, the limited amount of air on board would mean death to the crew. But if a craft from the other country was also in space, the ability for one to dock with the other could be a lifesaver.

It was a sane moment in what had been, at times, an insane space race. Between the late 1950s, when the little *Sputnik* bleeped around the Earth, to the co-operative venture of the mid-1970s, America's mood had switched from panic to triumph to co-existence, at least in Space. Indeed, NASA, at which the US Congress had unquestioningly thrown several billion dollars to fund the moon project, now began to struggle for cash. On Capitol Hill, the moment seemed to have passed. There would be another moon walk, there would be the awful disaster of Challenger, which blew itself and its crew to smithereens soon after launch, there would be

unmanned probes to Mars and beyond. But never again would there be the frantic scramble that had characterized the Mercury and Apollo programmes.

It was a scramble both glorious and desperate, as is so often the way with human endeavour. It ended, in terms of its own ambitions, with Armstrong's marvellous moment on the moon. But even that was only one side of the coin, for space travel was and is an activity that depends on the willingness of brave men to put their lives on the line. For me the most fascinating postscript of Apollo 11 is a fact that emerged long after Armstrong, Aldrin and Collins got home. When the *Eagle* landed, it had just 13 seconds of fuel left in its tank. Such are the margins between triumph and disaster.

The Munich Olympics 1972

Terror comes to sport: 11 athletes murdered at Olympic Games

THE 1970s WAS A DECADE OF
unprecedented terrorist disruption in world
affairs. Britain was preoccupied with the
activities of terrorists in Northern Ireland,
where the modern 'Troubles' had begun in
1969. But the Middle East was the base for
most of the terrorist attacks on the rest of the
world, as well as being the setting for the long
and bloody civil war in Lebanon. This was a
tragedy for a country whose capital, Beirut, was
once known as the Paris of the Middle East.
The region was also the launching pad for one
of the most shocking outrages of the entire
century. Although sport was already highly
politicized as countries vied for the kudos
attached to staging major events, it was not
until 1972 that a great sporting occasion was
hijacked for the purposes of gaining the
worldwide publicity that all terrorists seek.
The Munich Olympics of that year ought to
be remembered for the American swimmer
Mark Spitz, who won seven gold medals.
Instead they have gone into history as the
setting for a bloody massacre, perpetrated
by terrorists but made even worse by a
botched attempt to stop the culprits
getting away.

On the rest day between the end of the
swimming programme in which Spitz, an
American Jew, had starred, and the start of the
track and field events British television viewers
tuned in on the morning of 5 September and
will not easily forget what they saw. David
Coleman was fronting television coverage of
the Olympics from a BBC studio in Munich.
Coleman, a consummate sports broadcaster,

**A hooded terrorist
on the balcony outside
the rooms where the
athletes were held
hostage in the
Olympic village.**

Grand beginnings: the Munich Olympics opened to fanfares as the world's top athletes gathered in the packed stadium.

had suddenly turned into a news presenter when a band of guerrillas from an Arab movement called Black September burst into the Olympic village at dawn. Black September had been named after the month in 1970 when Palestinian paramilitaries were expelled from Jordan by King Hussein. Black September had soon become active, killing the Jordanian Prime Minister while he was visiting Cairo in November of 1971 and hijacking a Belgian passenger airliner in spring 1972. Indeed aircraft hijackings were one of the signature activities of Arab terrorism during the 1970s, activities that led to the tight security measures that are still in evidence at international airports today.

There had been tip-offs and intelligence warnings about a possible raid at Munich and 250 extra security men had been drafted in to the village as a precaution. Clearly that was not enough, for none of them saw the group of men, wearing dark clothing and hoods over their heads, scale a wall and start making their way towards the building where the Israeli team slept. At 5.10 a.m. they broke through the doors of the Israeli dormitory and began blazing away with sub-machine-guns, instantly killing Moshe Weinberg, a 33-year-old wrestling coach. Yosef Romano, a weightlifter, was mortally wounded after using his bulk to hold a door closed while two colleagues escaped through a window. The terrorists refused to let doctors into the building to treat Romano and he died within hours. Miraculously, given that they were all asleep when the terrorists burst in, 15 Israelis escaped, through doors and windows, but 10 were taken hostage. One of

those got away a few minutes later, sprinting down a corridor and weaving from side to side as the terrorists fired at him. He escaped completely unhurt.

What followed was in effect a siege, with the terrorists holding the hostages inside the building. Incredibly, it was not until late in the afternoon that the International Olympic Committee (IOC) finally decided that the terrorist attack was more important than volleyball and gymnastics. For five hours, various events had continued, with athletes from other countries leaving the village for their events, many of them unaware of the seriousness of the situation inside the Israeli building. Eventually, the IOC announced that the Games would stop for one day as a memorial. They

resumed the following day after a heated debate within the IOC, with some delegates arguing that the Games should be called off altogether while others successfully argued that doing that would give an even bigger victory to terrorism.

Immediately after the initial attack the Games village was surrounded by more than 10,000 armed police. Understandably enough, this slamming of the stable door after the horse had bolted did nothing to placate the Israelis, who were angry about lax security and said that, whatever the outcome of the hostage taking, the whole team would go home when it was over. That reaction and other comments underlined the fact that the attack could hardly have happened in a worse place at a worse

Four of the Israeli weightlifters pictured before the Games started. Only the one on the right survived the terrorist attack.

time. The Israeli team had been warmly welcomed to West Germany, as it then was, 30 years after World War II and the Holocaust. Now, once again, Jews were being massacred on German soil, only a few miles from the remains of the concentration camp at Dachau .

The German Interior Minister came to the Olympic Village and opened a dialogue with the terrorists. Willy Brandt, the West German Chancellor, flew to Munich from Bonn and took charge of the negotiations, which were already attracting controversy because there were those in both the German and Israeli governments – and especially the latter – who were opposed to negotiating with terrorists on principle. The Israeli Prime Minister, Mrs Golda Meir, insisted from the start that no Arab prisoners held in Israel would be released, and that remained the Israeli position throughout. However, the talks continued and television pictures showed a Palestinian, dressed in jacket and slacks and wearing a white hat, standing outside the Israeli headquarters animatedly talking to the negotiators, who were all in dark suits and ties. The Palestinian's body language, left arm thrust forward, finger pointing, made it

eminently clear who had the whip hand.

The terrorists' basic demand was familiar from other such situations: they wanted their prisoners released and they wanted free passage out of Germany to an Arab country. The Tunisian ambassador to Bonn and officials from the Arab League's office in West Germany tried to mediate with the terrorists, without much sign of success. At one stage, two politicians from the German Interior Ministry offered themselves as hostages in place of the Israeli athletes, but the offer was turned down; Black September knew the publicity value of having Israeli hostages. Various deadlines were imposed, accompanied by threats that some or all of the hostages would be killed if the deadline was not met. As each deadline approached, it was put back. This game of bluff and counter-bluff went on all day.

While the talking continued, the German authorities considered what to do. There was some support for storming the compound but the idea was soon rejected as too dangerous. If the fact that Jewish athletes were involved was not sufficient as a reminder of the echoes from World War II, there was another factor that weighed in the equation. After the war, West Germany had not been allowed to re-arm, nor had it wanted to. The country was determined to maintain the lowest possible military profile and that extended to its lack of special anti-terrorist forces which, although they existed by the time of the Munich attack, were generally regarded as being of lesser quality than units such as the Special Air Service (SAS) in Britain. The whole approach to security at Munich had

in mind sensitivities about German militarism and there were many observers who felt that such an approach unwittingly gave an opening to Arab terrorists

As day turned into night the authorities became more hopeful that the first objective in their strategy for dealing with the terrorists, which was to get them away from the Olympic village, was achievable. It became apparent that some sort of deal had been struck and shortly after 9 p.m. the terrorists agreed to leave the Olympic compound. The Arab commandos showed that they had been well trained, and terrorist experts watching the events unfold noted that before moving to an airfield, the hostages were split into two groups. Their hands were tied and they were blindfolded. Two helicopters appeared and flew the terrorists, with their hostages, to Furstenfeld, a German military base about 20 miles from Munich. A Boeing 727 commercial aircraft had been made ready for the use of the Arabs. The helicopter landed on the airfield and, just before midnight, the terrorists and the hostages began the walk from the landing point to the Boeing.

Both the terrorists and the Germans knew that this was the one opportunity the authorities would have to intervene. Privately, the Germans had made it clear all day that, having allowed the terrorists on to their territory and into the Olympic village, there

was no way they would be allowed to get away. But an operation in the dark, at an airfield, against experienced hostage takers, carried huge risks. This was the acid test, the moment when the Germans could save some of the face they had lost by allowing the Olympic village to be breached in the first place. Sharpshooters were already in position along the path between the helicopters and the Boeing. Suddenly, all the ancilllary lights around the airfield went out and, just as suddenly, German special forces opened fire. The guerrillas and the first group of hostages were already well away from the first helicopter and, as the shots rang out, the terrorists started shooting the hostages. The second group was only just leaving the second helicopter. One of the terrorists started shooting, another threw a grenade into the second helicopter, blowing it

Armed police
carrying automatic
weapons drop into
positions opposite the
Israeli team
quarters.

Munich city police was also killed. The pilot of one of the helicopters is badly injured.' The next day, in a break from frantic talks as to whether the Olympics would continue, the President of the IOC, Avery Brundage, spoke at a special service to remember the dead: 'Every civilized person recoils in horror at the barbarous, criminal intrusion of terrorists into peaceful Olympic precincts. We mourn our Israel friends, victims of this brutal assault. The Olympic flag, and the flags of all the world, fly at half mast. Sadly, in this imperfect world, the greater and the more important the Olympic Games become, the more they open to commercial, political and now criminal pressures.'

In saying this Brundage had hit several nails on the head at once, for there were plenty of people who would wonder whether an ever larger, ever more commercialized and politicized Olympic movement was worth it if another Munich might be the price. The repercussions of what happened at Munich were to be felt for many years, in the Olympic movement and in the wider world, and indeed they are still being felt. The Israeli government and people were furious, not just that the athletes died but about the fact that security — understandably both an Israeli obsession and an Israeli speciality — had not been of the highest order at Munich. The tragic irony was that low-key security had been a deliberate

and its occupants to smithereens. Four of the guerrillas and a Munich policeman were killed in the gun battle. Three terrorists were captured at the airport but when the airfield fell silent and the lights were put on again, it became apparent that the rescue attempt had ended in tragedy: all nine hostages were dead.

Soon after the shoot-out a spokesman for the German government gave a briefing, in English. It was for most people the first intimation that a tragedy had turned into a disaster and it was broadcast by BBC Radio: 'Although we had put up lights and tried to light the whole premises, it was not possible that we could shoot at first go all the terrorists. The others, as they had threatened, opened fire on the hostages, on the helicopter and also on the airport buildings. In the process the hostages were killed and one policeman of the

'The mysticism and magic of the Olympic movement were lost in the aftermath of Munich. You went from idealism and romanticism to the Games of big business.'

This change was in some measure simply a product of the modern era but there is no question that the decision to continue with the Munich Olympics after athletes had been killed, although easy enough to justify in rational terms, gave the impression that 'the show must go on' was a slogan that had now moved from Broadway to encompass the sports arena. And there were those who asked what the scale of the public outcry might be if a Broadway show went on after 11 of the cast members had just been killed.

If sport changed after Munich there were other consequences of the massacre, some immediate, some much longer-term. There was certainly an increase in terrorist incidents, including one directly linked to Munich. On 29 October, less than eight weeks after the massacre, another Black September group hijacked a German Lufthansa Boeing 727 as it flew over Turkey. Carrying pistols and hand grenades, the hijackers demanded that the

policy, used, along with jolly music and pastel colours, to give Germany and the German people a modern, friendly image during the Games. There are many who regard Munich as a turning point in the history of sport and certainly the Olympic Games took on a much more obvious political aspect after Munich than it had before. There would be boycotts: by the black African nations at Montreal in 1976 and by the United States and others at Moscow in 1980, with a tit-for-tat boycott of Los Angeles in 1984 by the Soviet bloc countries.

The documentary film maker Bud Greenspan directed *Triumph and Tragedy*, the official film of the Munich Olympics. He said:

three terrorists captured at Munich be released. The West German government, fearing another massacre of innocents, gave in. The decision brought a fresh wave of criticism from Israel, where relatives of the dead athletes were already planning legal action against the German government. These actions were to go on for many years and it was only in May 1996 that the last two actions came before a court in Munich, where they were thrown out on a technicality. A class action had been filed two years earlier by 29 relatives of the dead athletes, seeking $29 million in damages from the Munich authorities and the federal and state governments.

There were other long-term consequences that had a more human, hopeful touch than the dry proceedings of a courtroom. Mark Spitz, the great swimmer whose achievements at Munich had been overshadowed by the massacre, was invited to Israel for the Maccabiah Games 13 years after Munich. Spitz had competed twice in the Maccabiah Games, which, like the Olympics, take place every four years. In 1985, with his swimming career long since finished, he was invited to carry the torch into the stadium and light the flame that, again like the Olympics, burns throughout the event. Spitz ran into the darkened stadium carrying the torch and as he did so, three children, little girls, ran with him. Each of their fathers had died in the massacre at Munich.

The Birth of the First Test Tube Baby | 1978

Louise Brown, the first test tube baby, comes into the world in Oldham general hospital, Lancashire.

THE BIRTH OF ANY BABY IS A great event in someone's life, rarely is the birth of a baby a significant event in all our lives. Late in the evening of 25 July 1978, a blue-eyed baby with a frizz of blonde hair emerged into the world at Oldham general hospital in Lancashire. Louise Brown was delivered by caesarean section and weighed in at 5 pounds and 12 ounces, but her appearance, weight and method of delivery were not what made Louise special. She was the world's first test tube baby. An egg from her mother, Lesley, who was sterile because of blocked fallopian tubes, had been fertilized in a test tube using sperm from her father. The embryo was then implanted in the mother and the pregnancy proceeded normally, except that it was attended by a blitz of publicity. A few hours after the birth Patrick Steptoe, a pioneer of research in the field, announced to a scrum of reporters and cameramen: 'All examinations showed that the baby is quite normal. The mother's condition after delivery was also excellent'. Louise Brown's financial condition at birth could be similarly described, for a newspaper had paid £300,000 for exclusive rights to her story.

Within a few years of the extraordinary events at Oldham, artificial insemination by various means was to become commonplace. There were legitimate moral questions to be debated and some moralists argued that anything other than conception through intercourse between two people in a loving marriage was unacceptable. The contrary argument was and remains that a woman

Doctors stun world as IVF opens
new medical era

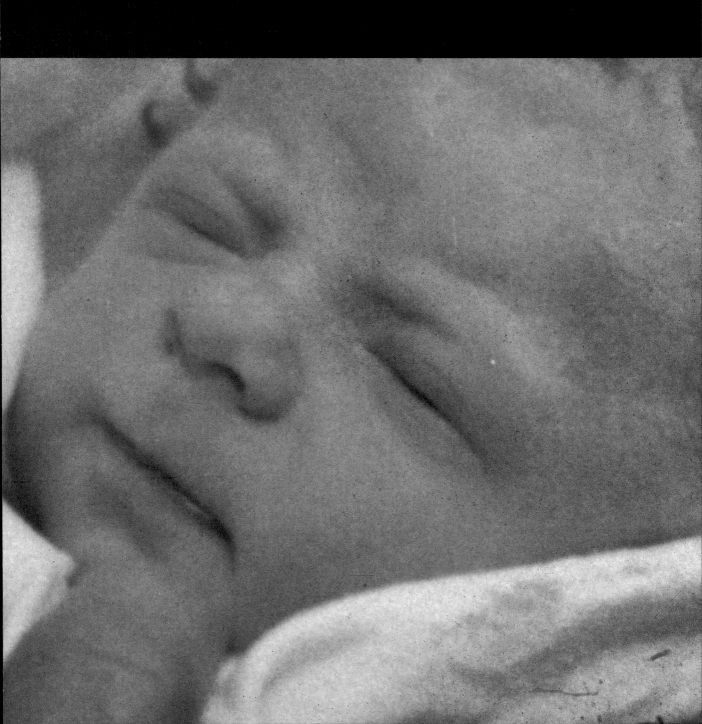

The Doctors behind the Louise Brown miracle: Patrick Steptoe (left) and Robert Edwards.

should not be prevented from having children just because of some bodily malfunction that made normal conception impossible. This debate would continue for many years but it was soon to be joined by medical developments that made the creation of a baby in a test tube seem routine. Among other difficulties, the issue was to become politicized.

A graphic example of the complications that can arise from such medical developments came in America in 1997. By that time, in vitro fertilization (IVF) – in vitro is Latin for 'in glass', a reference to eggs being developed in a laboratory dish – had moved on from the relative simplicity of the Brown case, in which both natural parents contributed to the embryo, to more complex examples where anonymous donors were used. In September of 1997, the case of two-year-old Jaycee Louise Buzzanca came before a court in California. John and Luanne Buzzanca had spent several years trying for a child without success. In 1994 they paid a fertility clinic to combine an egg with sperm from a couple who acted as anonymous donors. The process was successful and the embryo was implanted in a woman acting as a surrogate mother, another practice that was becoming as widespread as it was controversial. A month before Jaycee was born, John Buzzanca petitioned for divorce and in the course of a preliminary court hearing he said that he would not provide child support. It was the issue of child support that brought the matter to court, where the judge ruled that John was not the legal father and therefore could not be obliged to support the child. He

also ruled that Luanne was not the legal mother, though he suggested that that problem could be overcome if Luanne adopted Jaycee. But from whom? The anonymous genetic parents? The surrogate mother and her husband? At one stage the surrogate mother tried to claim the baby herself on the grounds that she had agreed to deliver a baby for a couple, whose divorce meant that the terms of the deal had been broken. However, this claim was subsequently withdrawn. The grim reality was that Jaycee had six parents: the Buzzancas, the surrogate mother and her husband and the anonymous genetic parents. Yet at the same time Jaycee had no parents.

If the rapid growth of IVF raised complex legal and moral questions, it also prompted much consideration of fertility itself. Why were so many people having problems giving birth to children in the 'normal' way? One part of the answer lay in the arrival of the birth pill, which became available on the National Health

Service in Britain in 1967. The pill undoubtedly gave women more control over their bodies but it coincided with much greater equality, and greater opportunity, for women in the workplace. That was undoubtedly a good thing but it meant that women increasingly tended to delay having children so that they could establish their careers first. Unfortunately later pregnancy can mean a greater likelihood of problems. In the United States, the number of women of childbearing age having fertility problems rose between 1988 and 1995 from 4.9 million to more than 6 million, a 25 per cent increase. But it takes two to create a child, and there is convincing evidence of a significant fall in the sperm count of males in the industrialized world, much of the blame placed, by scientists, at the door of pollution and chemical additives in food. But of course the fact that men were leaving fatherhood until later may also have come into the equation.

As these factors interfered with the

biological ability to have children, the psychological desire to procreate showed no sign of abating. With these two vital factors pulling in opposite directions, science was being asked to fill the gap. IVF was to become one of the key methods and by 1994 in the United States, there were more than 7,000 births a year using IVF. The moral questions, far from fading away, were to become ever more complex. If a woman who could not conceive naturally was entitled to have a child, what about a homosexual couple? Were two men, or two women, living together in a loving relationship, entitled to have children via surrogates? If they were, did this mean that same sex couples could also adopt? If not, was society punishing their sexuality by not allowing them to having children? These were huge issues and by the 1990s they had become an area of expertise for lawyers.

There would also be arguments as between different forms of IVF. The Louise Brown case had been straightforward, for the problem her parents faced was more technical than anything else. Surrogacy, which at one point threatened to become an industry itself, made the issue more complicated. But at least surrogates were serving a specific need at the time that it was needed: the controversy surrounding surrogates had more to do with whether they should be allowed to accept payment, as opposed to expenses. But what about sperm and egg banks? How legitimate was it to store the raw materials of creation, awaiting the right 'customer'? In October of 1997, a patient at a fertility clinic in Atlanta, Georgia, gave birth to

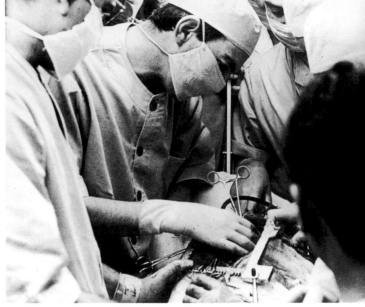

twin boys. The twins had developed from the eggs of another woman, taken two years before and frozen at the clinic. This was the first birth of its kind anywhere in the world. There had been plenty of attempts to freeze and then thaw a woman's eggs but, because eggs are more fragile than male sperm, all had failed. The Atlanta success, with a woman who had agreed to take part in the experiment on condition her name was never revealed, made headlines everywhere and brought a flood of calls to the clinic.

Egg freezing opened yet another fertility frontier. The technique meant that if a woman was facing surgery that would threaten her chances of having a child naturally, she could have eggs removed in advance and frozen until she was fit enough to go through a pregnancy. Freezing opened another possibility directly related to the tendency for women to delay having children until their careers were established. The risks of late childbirth would perhaps be obviated or reduced if a woman's eggs were removed and frozen when she was young and then implanted later when she decided to have a family. The possibilities were almost endless, which was precisely what worried a lot of people who felt that the desirable was being overtaken by the possible.

If reproduction was to prove the most dramatic and controversial area of medical advance in the late twentieth century it was by no means the only one. Medical science had

been finding ways to obviate the effects of bodily malfunction for many years before IVF came along. Transplant surgery gave new hope to thousands of people with diseased organs, and the techniques were already being developed before the end of World War II. In the early 1940s, a Russian surgeon, Vladimir Demikar, transplanted a new heart and lungs into a dog. In 1962, the heart of a chimpanzee was given to a human for the first time, though it functioned only for a few days. There was an important technical breakthrough for transplant surgery in the mid-1960s when it was discovered that matching tissue between donor and recipient vastly improved the chances of the transplant working. That research assisted in the great leap forward for transplant surgery in 1967. On 3 December a team of 30 doctors

(Below) Louis Washkansky, the first human heart transplant patient, shortly after Christian Barnard carried out the operation in Cape Town.

and nurses at the Groote Schuur hospital in Cape Town, South Africa, announced that they had carried out the world's first transplant of a human heart.

The team was led by Dr Christian Barnard, a professor of cardiothoracic surgery. The recipient was Louis Washkansky, a 53-year-old grocer, who was given the heart of Denise Darvall, a 25-year-old bank clerk who had been rushed to the hospital after a car accident. She had been fatally injured but lived long enough to give permission for her heart to be removed and transplanted. The operation lasted for five hours and it turned Barnard into an

international superstar. As he put it: 'On Saturday, I was a surgeon in South Africa, very little known. On Monday, I was world renowned.' The media flocked to the hospital and Barnard's subsequent fame was helped by the fact that he was handsome and only 45 years old. News bulletins in Britain, as everywhere else, led with the breakthrough and Barnard appeared on the covers of magazines all over the world. The son of a poor Afrikaner preacher on South Africa's Great Karroo Plateau, Barnard had trained at the University of Cape Town. He became fascinated by the possibilities of heart surgery while he was at the University of Minnesota, where he began helping researchers who were developing a heart-lung machine. Barnard switched from general surgery to cardiology and cardiothoracic (heart-lung) surgery.

Back in South Africa he carried out a number of successful heart transplants using dogs, like the Russian Demikar. When Denise Darvall was admitted to the hospital, Barnard knew the chance had arrived to try a human transplant. Washkansky had diabetes and advanced heart disease: he was dying. The transplant, Barnard felt, had an 80 per cent chance of success. He wrote later: 'For a dying man it is not a difficult decision because he knows he is at the end. If a lion chases you to the bank of a river

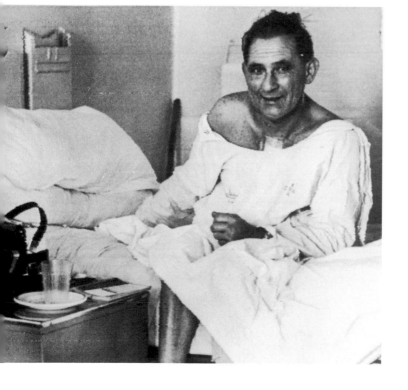

filled with crocodiles, you will leap into the water convinced you have a chance to swim to the other side. But you would never accept such odds if you knew there was no lion.' The operation was a surgical success but Washkansky lived for only 18 days, dying of double pneumonia brought on by the fact that his immune system was functioning at such a low level. Professor M C Botha, an immunologist who worked on the transplant with Barnard, recalled going to the tearoom at the hospital when the operation was over. 'It was an extraordinary feeling, looking out at the cloudless clear morning,' he said. 'I had the feeling the openness was symbolic of something.'

Barnard toured the world, giving lectures and television and radio interviews. At the time

surgeons were not celebrities, but Barnard became a household name, the most celebrated medical man who had ever lived. There are downsides to wealth and fame and Barnard was to be divorced twice over the next dozen years. In 1983 he was forced to give up surgery because of rheumatoid arthritis. He wrote an autobiography and several novels, including a thriller set in the world of organ transplants. He moved from Cape Town to a 32,000 acre sheep farm in the Karroo region where he was brought up. His only further appearance in the public domain came in 1986 when he endorsed an anti-ageing cream which turned out to have little effect and which was subsequently withdrawn from the market.

If the spotlight had moved from Barnard,

Dolly the cloned sheep gets the star treatment from the world's press.

and indeed from transplants – which soon became commonplace, if not routine – the beam of publicity and controversy would not take many years to find a new focus. Already genetic engineering, which theoretically enabled science to remove genes that caused certain illnesses or even certain types of behaviour, had become the subject of major controversy. Now came a variant of genetic engineering in the form of cloning. In February 1997 the world's media descended on Roslin, near Edinburgh in Scotland, to take pictures of the latest scientific superstar, Dolly the sheep. Dolly was a clone. She was named after the country music star Dolly Parton and she was the creation of Dr Ian Wilmut of the Roslin Institute, working in partnership with PPL Therapeutics.

Dr Wilmut and Alan Colman of PPL were quick to counter the notion, rapidly spread in sections of the press, that this was science gone mad. 'These animals are absolutely normal sheep,' Colman said. 'They behave like sheep, they look like sheep. They are not genetic mutants.' But if sheep could be cloned, surely the same applied to humans? Dr Wilmut, who had cloned Dolly from a single mammary cell taken from a six-year-old ewe and then frozen, said that, although human cloning might be theoretically possible: 'We would find it ethically

completely unacceptable and we would not do it'. Others in the medical community were not so sure about cloning and Richard Nicholson of the *Bulletin of Medical Ethics* said: 'We may be sowing the seeds of our own destruction'. Dolly was soon to have plenty of other clones for company, including ten identical calves born in New Zealand the same year.

The implications of cloning led to all sorts of bizarre possibilities being advanced, and not just in the general press. A month after Dolly appeared, an article appeared in the learned magazine *New Scientist* that carried the startling headline: 'Will cloned cows rise from the dead?' The article reported on work by a team of scientists in Denmark, who were using genetic material from dead cows to create clones.

This raised the possibility of tissue from dead humans being used in cloning, which in turn meant that people might effectively be brought back from the dead.

The Danish process took immature, unfertilized eggs from the dead cows and emptied them of their DNA content. Next they took adult cells from the cows' ovaries. Then they fused the two together using an electric current. After a week, the fused cell grew into an embryo that was then implanted into a live cow, the clone's 'foster mother'.

Although much of the debate surrounding these extraordinary developments was hysterical, rational voices were also to be heard. It was pointed out, for example, that identical twins are no more than clones of each other, the only – though important – difference being that identical twins occurred naturally whereas cloning involved the active manipulation of a natural process. The atmosphere surrounding cloning calmed down somewhat when it was demonstrated that cloning could have benefits for those involved in IVF, thus bringing us back to where this chapter started. In May 1998 *New Scientist* reported that a baby had been born after screening that used a procedure based on the same nuclear transfer technology that is at the root of cloning.

Although IVF had seemed, when it was first developed, to answer all the prayers of infertile couples, many of them were to be disappointed. IVF is affected by the same natural problems that afflict any birth, particularly the tendency of most embryos to contain either too many or too few chromosomes. IVF technicians test some cells from embryos for genes that can cause illnesses such as cystic fibrosis or Down's Syndrome. But to test all chromosomes would take too long: an embryo must be placed in the uterus within a day or so of fertilization, whereas the chromosome tests can take a week. However, the nuclear transfer procedures used in cloning speed up the procedure so that the tests can be completed within a few hours. Such developments demonstrate the closer relationship between many branches of research, so that what can be frightening in one context can be a life-saver – or life-giver – in another.

What is clear is that each development in medical research leads to new moral dilemmas. Or rather, they lead to a new expression of the same moral dilemma. And the real danger from the rapid progress of medical research may lie in the fact that it tends to leave behind the rest of society, in particular those who frame its laws. Procedures such as cloning are legal because they are not illegal rather than because society has made an active decision that cloning is desirable. No one has ever passed a law sanctioning IVF. There is no consensus as to whether there should be a limit to transplant surgery. We accept heart, lung and other organ transplants as routine and desirable, but how will we react to brain transplants? We cannot know. All we can know is what has been proven by medical science over the past century: that if it can be done, it will be done.

Gary Watson (on the right), an organic farmer from Devon, at a London protest against trials of genetically modified maize in 1998.

The Murder of John Lennon 1980

Autograph hunter murders former Beatle John Lennon outside his home

John Lennon at the height of The Beatles fame in 1967.

JOHN LENNON SAID IN AN INTERVIEW broadcast on Radio 1 shortly after his death that he felt safe living in New York, a remark that acquired a certain irony on the night of Monday 8 December 1980. Lennon emerged from a car outside the Dakota Apartments where he lived with Yoko Ono, his second wife, and walked up the steps to the door. As he did so a voice called to him from the street and he turned. The voice belonged to Mark David Chapman, whom Lennon had met for the first time a few hours earlier. Chapman had been standing on the sidewalk when Lennon left for a recording session. Chapman produced Lennon's new album, *Double Fantasy*, and asked the singer to sign it. Jack Douglas, Lennon's record producer, said later that they had spent the evening at the Record Plant studios in mid-town Manhattan. They left at about 10.30 p.m. Lennon was going to get something to eat and then go home. He arrived back outside the Dakota building, which was opposite Central Park, shortly before 11 p.m., six hours after he had left. Chapman was still there, but now he was not carrying a record album, he was carrying

a gun. It was a Charter Arms .38 revolver containing five rounds of ammunition. Chapman took up a combat stance and emptied all five bullets into Lennon, who staggered up the steps into the apartment building's entrance, calling out: 'I'm shot'. He then collapsed on the floor.

When the police arrived Chapman was still standing outside the building. Lennon was rushed to the St Luke's-Roosevelt hospital but he died shortly after arriving there. 'There was blood all over the place' a hospital worker told reporters. Chapman was put in the back of a police car, taken into custody, charged with murder and subsequently convicted. There appeared to be no particular motive, though there were various claims, including one that Chapman had been ordered to kill Lennon by God. It also emerged that Chapman had been seen hanging around outside the apartments on the two days before the killing. He had only recently arrived in New York from Hawaii, where he bought the gun, and had stayed at the YMCA for two nights before moving to the Sheraton Centre hotel in Manhattan.

When Chapman was taken in by police, he

had in his pockets a copy of JD Salinger's *The Catcher in the Rye* and 14 hours of Beatles music on cassette tapes. He was not carrying the *Double Fantasy* album that Lennon had autographed for him; Chapman described later how he had stashed the album behind a watchman's booth before he carried out the shooting. Chapman was put on trial for the murder and given a sentence of 20 years-to life. His defence lawyers had begged him to plead not guilty by reason of insanity but Chapman insisted on a guilty plea. He seemed to revel in having carried out the murder, though he never gave any clear reasons for doing it. In a rambling 1981 interview, soon after the trial, Chapman cited Salinger's classic novel of teenage angst as having a vital bearing on his life: 'I was in a mental hospital for two

years. It was there where I found *The Catcher in the Rye*. I hadn't finished the first chapter when I noticed that the man said in the book the things I never could. The answers for all my questions were there. It was incredible, it was like God's revelation.' None of which even came close to explaining why Chapman had shot Lennon. Perhaps he didn't know himself.

The murder of Lennon was a tremendous shock and not just because he was only 40 years old. The Beatles, the Liverpool band that turned Lennon into a world celebrity, had broken up in acrimonious circumstances almost 10 years before Lennon died. And for five years, since 1975, Lennon had been a virtual recluse, dropping out of public life to spend more time with Yoko Ono and their son, Sean. Lennon turned himself into a househusband, tending the family home and cooking most of the meals. Those who knew him in the early days would have regarded this new role with amusement, for Lennon had been a hard-nosed rocker in a leather jacket who never gave much sign of knowing what an oven looked like, never mind how one might heat it up. Lennon had re-emerged into the public gaze, just a month before the shooting, with the new album, *Double Fantasy*, co-written with Yoko Ono. He was struck down on the brink of another career, unlikely to be as successful as the first but nonetheless certain to put him back in the record charts.

The world had become used to prematurely dead rock stars but usually they died of drink, drugs or in accidents. The violent manner of Lennon's departure, all the more poignant given his campaigns for peace, was to turn him into something close to a martyr. Nearly 20 years after he died, hundreds of Internet web sites still devote themselves to his memory. One, called 'The John Lennon Eternal Flame', burns a 'virtual candle' and, using a level of exaggeration that Lennon would have found hilarious, asks people to remember 'the greatest songwriter who ever walked on the face of this planet'. Another site, endorsed by Yoko Ono (who owns the trademark 'John Lennon') runs a John Lennon songwriting contest, which offers prizes in half a dozen categories, from rock to classical to jazz to hip-hop. The competition is even equipped with a 45-foot tour bus, fitted out as a mobile recording studio, which visits high schools and universities around the United States.

So who was this man, that 20 years after he died has a bus named after him and millions of fans who still buy his records and write letters to his widow? Lennon's story is of course indivisible from that of The Beatles, for his adult history is that of the group. Lennon was born in Liverpool in October 1940 into a working-class home that was not to be a home for long. When Lennon was four his parents split up. He lived with his mother for a time but she died and Lennon went to live with the person who would become vicariously famous many years later because her name often popped up in interviews: Aunt Mimi. Lennon was never reconciled to what his father had done by deserting the family and when his father surfaced after Lennon became famous he was firmly rejected: 'I don't feel as if I owe him anything,' Lennon said. 'He never helped me. I got there by myself.'

Neither his mother nor Aunt Mimi had the easiest of rides bringing up John, who was something of a prankster. Nor was he much good at the mainstream subjects in school, though he showed a certain talent for English and an even greater facility for art. His teachers noted that he seemed to enjoy drawing grotesque figures, even cripples. One teacher suggested that Lennon should go to the Liverpool College of Art, which he did and there he met Cynthia Powell, who was to become his first wife. But a partnership of a different kind was already forming and that was to prove the more significant from the standpoint of Lennon's career. Lennon and Paul McCartney met at a church social in 1955 and

soon began spending time in each other's houses, picking out guitar chords and writing songs. They formed a duo called The Quarrymen and three years after that first meeting, the duo became a trio when George Harrison joined them.

The group subsequently acquired a drummer, Pete Best, and became The Beatles. They played in various Liverpool clubs, notably the Cavern Club, and at the Star Club in Hamburg, Germany. Their musical influences came from the great rhythm and blues bands of America, whose records had been available to Lennon and McCartney when they were boys because merchant seamen brought the music back with them from the US. Rock music was still relatively new in Britain, the biggest home-grown star, Cliff Richard, having had his first hit, 'Move It', in 1958. But The Beatles were working on songs that were as far removed from Cliff Richard as could be imagined. The Beatles had several lucky breaks, the first of

them probably being the arrival of Brian Epstein as their manager. Epstein was no showbiz rip-off merchant. He genuinely liked the band and he had a special admiration for Lennon's somewhat wacky persona. Epstein, having seen various humdrum rock groups rise to fame, knew The Beatles needed to be distinctive and the best way to achieve that was to have a touch of class. Therefore he encouraged the famous mop top hair styles and the distinctive high-collar suits.

This is not the place for a history of The Beatles. Suffice it say that from their first hit, 'Please Please Me' in 1962 – by which time Ringo Starr had replaced Pete Best on drums – to the break-up of the band seven years later, the 'fab four' carried all before them. They were the first British rock act to make it big in the United States, at one stage having five singles in the *Billboard* top 50 simultaneously, an achievement not even Elvis Presley could match. They wrote an astonishing variety of

The 'fab four': from the left, McCartney, Starr, Harrison and Lennon.

sheer force of his personality, understood how this worked extremely well. When The Beatles topped the bill at a Royal Variety Performance,

Lennon stepped up to the microphone to ask the audience to join in. The people in the cheap seats, he said, could clap their hands while those in the 'posh seats' should 'rattle your jewellery'.

music, from out and out rock numbers such as 'I Wanna Hold Your Hand' to hauntingly beautiful ballads such as 'Eleanor Rigby' and 'Yesterday'. There were also aberrations, including a song called 'Maxwell's Silver Hammer', a jaunty number which appeared to be about a serial killer, and a nasty song called 'Run For Your Life' ('I'd rather see you dead little girl than to be with another man'). Still, the body of work was high quality and it sold like water in a desert.

If The Beatles had good fortune through the presence of Brian Epstein, they had further good fortune in their record producer, George Martin, a master of the art who also happened to be more interested in making music than making money. There was the usual quota of hangers on and exploiters around the band, but Epstein and Martin were not among them. Martin helped The Beatles pull off the trick of being both mainstream and fringe at the same time. Lennon, the leader of the band through

the audience, which could scarcely tell whether it was being mocked or patronized, wasn't bothered either way: they loved it. A band that was supposed to be one of the icons of rebellious youth, a band that by the mid-1960s was into drugs, Indian mystics and cheeky encounters with politicians, had somehow contrived to become loveable. Establishment recognition came formally in 1965 when the four were awarded the MBE, though Lennon subsequently returned his as a protest against the war in Vietnam.

Lennon had a less easy ride with public and press than did The Beatles as a group. A tremendous hate-fest was launched in the tabloid press when Lennon remarked that The

Beatles were 'more popular than Jesus Christ', a statement that was both absurd and true at the same time. Absurd because the comparison was meaningless, true because, at the height of their fame, there were probably more Beatles fans than Christians in the world. But so what? The remark served as a reminder that, whereas Lennon was indeed a good songwriter with a certain amount of off-the-wall ability as a writer of comic prose, he was not exactly a philosophical giant. But if there was any doubt that the band would take a place in the history of music, it was expunged by the seminal 1967 album *Sgt Pepper's Lonely Hearts Club Band*, widely regarded as pop music's first 'concept' album. It was not really that, for the record had no theme, but the writing and arranging took popular music into territory previously unexplored.

The inevitable collapse of the group came in 1970 amid a good deal of acrimony and infighting. The relationship between Lennon and McCartney became strained almost to breaking point. There were those who blamed the influence of two women, McCartney's wife, the former Linda Eastman, and Lennon's second wife, Yoko Ono, whom Lennon had married in 1969. Typically, Lennon and Ono put their wedding and the honeymoon in reverse order. 'We went to Paris on our honeymoon,' Lennon said, 'then interrupted our honeymoon to get married on the rock of Gibraltar.'

Of the two 'Beatles women', Ono was certainly the more controversial. Much of the antipathy towards her in Britain had the ugly smack of xenophobia, for Ono was not only an avant-garde artist but she was also Japanese (Linda Eastman, an American, appeared to be more acceptable). Lennon once complained in a British television interview that parts of the press had been cruel towards Ono, calling her 'ugly'. Lennon said that normally the press called even ugly people 'attractive', but in Ono's case no such euphemism was applied. The underlying problem had nothing to do with Ono's looks – she was certainly not ugly – but there was a perception that Ono was an undue and undesirable influence on Lennon and that it was she, directly or indirectly, who caused the break-up of the group. A simpler explanation was more likely the true one: the band had simply reached the end of its useful life. Lennon said in an interview a few months before he was shot that he had wanted to leave the group in 1966, but 'just didn't have the guts'.

When the band did fall apart, the problem for its former members what to do next? If you are starting at the top, where do you go? Lennon moved to New York and continued writing songs. McCartney formed a new band, Wings. The songs Lennon and McCartney wrote separately tended to reflect their Beatles input, with McCartney concentrating on the sort of melodies that stayed in the mind while Lennon produced a harder-edged, more cynical output. But they each had a feel for melody, as Lennon demonstrated with 'Woman' – inevitably dubbed 'Lennon's "Yesterday"' – and the title song from his first post-Beatles album, *Imagine*. For the same album, he wrote one song, 'How Do You Sleep?' that mocked McCartney's 'pop' style and which Lennon

would later regret, though it was said at the time to have been a response to various 'hidden messages' in McCartney tracks. The feud, if that is what it was, had become silly. There were all sorts of legal and contractual disputes being fought out by lawyers and accountants over The Beatles' fortune, but for Lennon to record a song that personalized the acrimony struck most people as crass. But the moment soon passed and Lennon seemed at

last to have developed a persona separate from the group, though he would be labelled a 'former Beatle' right up to the moment of his death. But he and Ono managed to strike out in new directions. 'Peace and Love' became his slogan and Lennon, always with Ono at his side, appeared at various peace festivals, starting with Toronto in 1969. The pair formed the Plastic Ono band and did various concerts for charity. The band's last appearance was at a

The following year Lennon and Ono separated. Lennon was to refer to this as his 'lost weekend', though it lasted more than a year. Lennon went to Los Angeles, started drinking and going to parties and generally behaving like a rock star. He made a few records of his own and worked on tracks with Ringo Starr and David Bowie. Lennon got something out of his system in LA, for after 14 months he returned to Ono in New York. In 1975 Lennon simply dropped out of sight so far as the public was concerned. He was determined to play a full part in bringing up his new son, Sean, and threw himself into the task with relish. Clearly, he was a 'new man' ahead of his time. Lennon

remarkable gig in New York's Madison Square Garden in 1972. At that time, protests against the American war in Vietnam were at their height and the feminist movement was in full swing. The concert became a celebration of both these movements and ended with half the audience on stage, singing the Lennon anthem 'Give Peace A Chance'. The singing even continued outside the hall, with some of the audience marching along Fifth Avenue.

always denied that he had become a recluse and he was certainly seen around New York. But it was to be five years before he returned to the recording studio to record *Double Fantasy*. The album, which contained a track called 'Just Like Starting Over', was released just before he was shot.

There were several bizarre postscripts to the Lennon murder, one of which would surely have inspired a whole album of songs from

Lennon himself. Shortly after the shooting, a photograph surfaced which showed Lennon signing the *Double Fantasy* album outside his apartment. In the background stands Mark Chapman. The fact that the photograph was taken is not especially unusual, for there were a number of Lennon fans outside the building at the time and most of them would have been taking photographs. However, 18 years after the murder, in August 1998, the album that Lennon signed was put up for sale on the Internet at an asking price of $1.8 million. The album was offered anonymously by a man who picked it up at the scene of the crime after Lennon had been shot. The man had given it to the police who checked it for forensic evidence and then returned it to him. The auction was odd enough, even odder was the fact that a sharp New York lawyer contacted Chapman, who is in the Attica Correctional Facility in upstate New York, and told him that he had a right to 'assert a claim' to the album as a personal pos session. Chapman, who is serving a minimum 20-year sentence for the murder – he is eligible to apply for parole in October 2000 – said he would not be making a claim. Chapman told a local newspaper, the *Rochester Democrat and Chronicle*: 'I have no interest whatsoever in making such a claim. I have never profited from this crime and I never will. I hope the money will be donated to charity.'

The album eventually sold for $400,000. Wherever the money went, the auction itself demonstrated that Beatles memorabilia knows no limits of taste. One illustration of the way the Lennon and McCartney legend endures lies in the many thousands of cover records that they have inspired, their music having been recorded by everything from barber shop quartets to symphony orchestras to rap singers to opera divas.

There is even a vast number of novelty records based on Beatles tracks, with one man in England having a collection of 7,000. One of these is by a 'group' called The Beatle Bleaters. It consists of a collection of dogs, goats and cats barking, bleating and miaowing to the tune of 'Love Me Do'. You can't help feeling that John Lennon would have enjoyed that.

The Falklands War 1982

Falklands invasion sends Britain to war in the South Atlantic

Flying the flag: British troops march into Port Stanley to receive the Argentine surrender.

WHILE THE FALKLAND ISLANDERS slept through a grey dawn on Friday 2 April 1982, Argentine frogmen and commandos in rubber dinghies came ashore close to Port Stanley, capital of the remote islands, a British outpost in the south Atlantic. The first group of invaders took control of the lighthouse at the entrance to the harbour and other forces moved on to the airport. Helicopters whirred overhead and landed more troops at various strategic points around the town. At about 6 a.m., the Argentine commandos attacked Moody Brook barracks, which housed the single company of British Royal Marines on the island. Within a couple of hours, Rex Hunt, Britain's Governor, came to the conclusion that resistance was futile. There were by now more than 1,200 Argentine troops on the island. Hunt ordered a surrender. By 8.30 a.m., Argentina had control of the Falklands.

The initial news of the invasion, relayed to Britain via news broadcasts that morning, sounded almost comic. To the extent that

Argentina meant anything in Britain, it stood for beef and football. To the extent that the Falklands meant anything, they summoned dim memories of school lessons about Britain's former Empire. Few people knew how Britain had come to acquire the Falklands, fewer still knew why, or whether, the islands mattered. The air of comedy was reinforced by the fact that there had been a hint that something was up several days before the invasion when a group of Argentine scrap metal dealers occupied the Falklands out-island of South Georgia, hoisted the Argentine flag and went away. Anyone who had read Evelyn Waugh's *Scoop* began to think that this had the look of a conflict invented for the purposes of satire. If so, this impression was soon to be removed by the British Prime Minister, Margaret Thatcher.

Governor Hunt was flown out of the Falklands to Uruguay and thence to London. The Royal Marines were also sent home. Argentina appointed an army general in Hunt's stead and declared Las Malvinas, the Argentine

century. Modern negotiations over the islands had begun, at the insistence of the UN, in 1965. The issue was who had sovereignty over the islands, which cover an area the size of Wales, and their 1,800 inhabitants, most of whom lived off sheep farming.

Whatever the rights and wrongs of the sovereignty issue, the first casualty of the Falklands war was to be the British Foreign Secretary Lord Carrington, who resigned three days after the invasion saying: 'I accept responsibility for a very great national humiliation'. Two other Foreign Office ministers, Humphrey Atkins and Richard Luce, also went but Mrs Thatcher rejected an offer of resignation from John Nott, the Defence Secretary. Carrington was a diplomat of the old school and it was generally felt that he had taken responsibility, rather than being to blame. As such his departure was one of the more honourable resignations of modern times.

By the time Carrington went plans to re-take the Falklands were already well advanced. Thatcher, who had become Britain's first woman Prime Minister in 1979, was furious about the invasion. The midnight oil was burned at the Ministry of Defence from the moment the Argentines invaded and a task force was hastily organized. On Saturday 3 April, the United Nations Security Council debated the Falklands, passing a vote calling for an immediate withdrawal of the Argentine forces and the start of negotiations. On the same day, the British House of Commons gathered in emergency session to hear Thatcher announce the setting-up of the task force (indeed some

name for the islands, to be Argentine territory. There was dancing and cheering outside the Casa Rosada presidential palace in Buenos Aires, the Argentine capital, which was itself a novel event given the suppression imposed by the ruling military junta. General Galtieri, the junta's leader, broadcast to the people of the Falklands (most of whom were, and remain, holders of British passports) telling them that their safety was not under threat and that he wanted 'peaceful relations' with Britain. The invasion was plainly a breach of international law, although it was to emerge as the days passed that the Argentine government had for some years been pressing Britain, through negotiations at the United Nations in New York, to allow Argentina's claim to the islands. The ownership of the Falklands had been in dispute since Britain seized them in 1833. Britain claimed that it had been entitled to take the islands because they had been discovered and occupied by the British in the eighteenth

ships were already at sea) and that the government was determined 'to see the islands returned to British administration'.

Two days later, on 5 April, the task force began leaving Portsmouth and Plymouth amid scenes of patriotic fervour not witnessed since World War II. Families and well-wishers lined the dockside at the two great naval ports, cheering and waving flags. The aircraft carriers *Invincible* and *Hermes*, crammed with Harrier jump jets, left Portsmouth and various commercial vessels, including the *QE2*, were being hastily converted to carry troops. There were destroyers, frigates, troop transports and countless other vessels. Several submarines had already left for the south Atlantic. There was some disquiet about the fact that the Falklands was 8,000 miles by sea from Britain, whereas the islands were only 400 miles from Argentina, a country which had relatively sophisticated military hardware, including French Exocet missiles.

The press, especially the tabloid press and particularly the *Sun*, found a bellicose headline for every occasion and thus fed the national fervour. When the Argentines tried conciliation, the *Sun* thundered: 'STICK IT UP YOUR JUNTA'. As the ships sailed on, the newspapers ran campaigns supporting 'our brave lads', assisting a mood of national pride that at times reached Churchillian proportions. At Ascension Island in the mid-Atlantic, the ships that had sailed from Britain met with 18 other Royal Navy vessels that had been on exercise near Gibraltar. It would take the task force a total of two weeks to reach the Falklands and in this time there were those who hoped that diplomacy could stop the impending violence. The United States, although supporting Britain's position, was uneasy because it had been working for improved relations with Argentina, a key player in the South American 'sphere of influence' which was so important to Washington.

President Ronald Reagan, a close personal ally of Thatcher, offered both support and mediation, sending his Secretary of State, Alexander Haig, on a diplomatic mission to Buenos Aires and London, where he arrived on 8 April. Haig told the British that both sides should withdraw and some sort of interim administration should be put in to run the Falklands while the sovereignty issue was resolved. Britain said that the Argentines would have to withdraw first. Haig flew to Buenos Aires, where the junta insisted, among others things, on the British task force being turned around and on a British commitment to negotiate away sovereignty of the islands by a specific date. Haig knew this would not be acceptable in London and he was right. Haig

returned to Washington. There were further talks between Haig and Francis Pym, Carrington's successor as Foreign Secretary, but the diplomatic offensive was clearly not going to resolve the dispute. On 30 April, the US announced full support for Britain and imposed sanctions on the Argentines.

Before that, on 12 April, Britain established a military exclusion zone in a 320-kilometre arc around the Falklands. British submarines patrolled it and Argentina was told that any of its ships entering the zone was liable to attack. The zone was to be the unwitting cause of one of the war's great controversies when, on 2 May, the submarine HMS *Conqueror* torpedoed the Argentine cruiser *General Belgrano*, sinking it with the loss of 368 lives. Several issues arose, the key one being whether the *Belgrano* was sailing away from, or towards, the British ships in the area when it was attacked. The controversy has raged ever since but one certainty soon emerged: the sinking scuppered a late peace plan suggested by Peru and meant that a full-scale war was inevitable.

The *Belgrano* incident did Britain considerable harm in the eyes of the rest of the world. The first edition of the *Sun* on the morning after the sinking carried the huge front page headline: 'GOTCHA!' But what is less well known is that the ebullient Editor of the *Sun* at that time, Kelvin MacKenzie, removed the headline from subsequent editions when it became apparent that there had been a huge loss of life. Thatcher and her war cabinet had given specific approval for the sinking of the *Belgrano* but denied that the sinking was a deliberate attempt to escalate the war. The day after the incident, British people discovered that anyone who thought a war with Argentina would soon be over without any loss of life was making a serious mistake.

The loss of the *Belgrano* had fired up both the junta and the ordinary people of Argentina, whose forces set out to avenge the sinking. Two Super Etendard fighter jets, built by the French company Dassault and armed with Exocet anti-ship missiles, left the Argentine mainland behind and began heading east. It was 10.30 a.m. on Tuesday 4 May, although in the British Battle Group, which was stationed in the south-east section of the total exclusion zone, it was 1 p.m. That is because the Royal Navy uses 'Zulu', or Greenwich Mean Time, when at sea so that

the actions of ships are co-ordinated, wherever they may be, with their masters in London. The two fighters would be making an 860-mile round trip. When the two pilots were 150 miles out over the sea, they climbed to 15,000 feet and refuelled from a tanker aircraft. Then they flew on, losing height and lining themselves up to attack the British ships. They were travelling at 33 miles a minute. Meanwhile, on the outer fringe of the British fleet were three Type-42 guided missile destroyers, known in Navy parlance as 'picket ships'. On that day the picket ships, the most vulnerable in any fleet because they are always first to be attacked, were HMS *Coventry*, HMS *Glasgow* and HMS *Sheffield*.

The two fighters first appeared on British radar screens at 13.56 Zulu and then disappeared again; they had 'popped up'. Then the missiles fired by the fighters became visible on radar screen aboard *Glasgow*. Sea Dart missiles were fired to intercept the Exocets. There was a sense of relief aboard *Glasgow* as the crew realized that neither missile was going to hit their ship. One was headed harmlessly away, the other was headed straight for the *Sheffield*. Admiral Sandy Woodward recalls in *100 Days*, his superb account of the Falklands campaign, that *Sheffield* had two problems. At a critical moment, the ship had been transmitting on a satellite communications system, which had the effect of blotting out signals from the fighter aircrafts' radars. The second problem was that the significance of reports coming from HMS *Glasgow* were, for some reason, not fully appreciated aboard *Sheffield*.

The ship was doomed. On the bridge of the *Sheffield*, Lieutenant Peter Walpole and Lieutenant Brian Layshon spotted a smoke trail about a mile away. One of them grabbed a microphone: 'Missile attack! Hit the deck!' The Exocet struck the *Sheffield* amidships on the starboard side.

It made a large hole in the side of the ship, about 4 feet deep by 15 feet wide; a fire started and dense smoke began to billow out of the vessel and throughout its cramped quarters. A fire at sea is the worst nightmare known to man. And the fire was getting worse because it was being given leaking fuel to feed on. Several men died very early on, choked by the fumes. Helicopters from HMS *Hermes*, the flagship with Woodward on board, flew to assist the *Sheffield*. There was no water pressure on board the stricken destroyer so water had

to be flown in to fight the fires. Inflatable dinghies bobbed around the *Sheffield*, trying to help. She took a long time to die. The order to abandon ship came in the middle of the afternoon and the surviving crew members were taken off by helicopter and flown to the other frigates. *Sheffield* continued to burn, ever more fiercely. Sheets of paint fizzled and fell into the water. Twenty-one men died, another 24 were injured. But the key lesson of the *Sheffield* was perhaps best expressed by Admiral Woodward's wife, Charlotte, who was dining at the Cavalry Club in London when news that the *Sheffield* had been lost came in. 'As from that moment,' Mrs Woodward recalled, 'I rather stopped regarding the Argentinian navy as something out of Gilbert and Sullivan.'

There were to be other losses as the war went on, including the terrible destruction of the landing craft *Sir Galahad*. There would be acts of enormous bravery and sacrifices of life by troops as the campaign to retake the Falklands continued. But the *Sheffield* had a special significance because it was the first major shock of the Falklands war, bringing the realization in Britain that the availability of modern weaponry meant that the most sophisticated, well-equipped and well-trained forces were vulnerable. There was never any question that Britain had superior might, but the sinking of the *Sheffield* proved that no enemy could be taken for granted, or assumed to be impotent. The size and importance of the international arms industry had produced a

situation where a key British vessel had been destroyed by a missile and an aircraft, both made in a country, France, which millions of British people visited every summer.

In narrower terms the loss of the *Sheffield* demonstrated that the British task force lacked air cover. Extra Harrier jets arrived on 18 May but the Argentines still had more air power. The Argentine problem was range, because its jets could only just carry enough fuel to reach the British fleet and get back to base. That restricted their activities, but there would be more British losses, including, on 23 May, HMS *Antelope*. In the next two days, both HMS *Coventry* and HMS *Broadsword* were hit. On

25 May, the *Atlantic Conveyor*, a merchant ship carrying helicopters and other vital supplies, was hit by a cruise missile. These attacks happened in the stretch of water between the two main islands, East Falkland and West Falkland, which became known as 'bomb alley'.

Meanwhile British troops had already landed on the Falklands, at San Carlos, and now there was to be a further attack, on the Argentine garrison that was dug in at Goose Green. The battle began on 28 May, after the British forces had walked the 20 kilometres to Goose Green because the rugged terrain was useless for vehicles. There were 300 British troops from the 2nd Battalion the Parachute

Regiment and after some early advances they were pinned down by Argentine fire. Goose Green was the battle for which Colonel H. Jones, commander of 2 Para, was posthumously awarded the Victoria Cross after he launched an attack on an Argentine machine gun post. That was by no means the only act of courage that day and eventually the British trapped the Argentine garrison, which surrendered. A day or so later troops took one of the peaks above Port Stanley and the northern route into the capital was thereby secured. The early part of June was spent preparing to take Port Stanley, which was protected by about 9,000 Argentine soldiers. The British advance began on 11 June and troops secured the outer ring of hills by the next day. On 13 June, the Scots Guards took Mount Tumbledown after a fierce battle. The war was nearly over. British troops marched to the edge of Stanley, where they waited while their commanders spoke to their Argentine opposite numbers in the town. At 9 p.m. local time on 14 June, the Argentine surrender was signed and a white flag flew over Port Stanley, soon to be replaced by the Union Jack. Three days later, General Galtieri resigned and the military junta in Buenos Aires fell.

On the night of the surrender, members of the House of Commons gathered to hear Thatcher announce that the war was over. She said it had been won by an operation that was 'boldly planned, bravely executed and brilliantly accomplished'. There were cheers in the Commons. There were even more cheers in Downing Street, where Thatcher was greeted by crowds singing 'For she's a jolly good fellow'

as she returned from the Commons. She stepped out of her official car to tell the crowd: 'We had to do what we had to do. Britain is great again.'

About 1,000 lives were lost on the two sides in a war which ended with the dispute that was at its heart back at square one. A remote British outpost had been reclaimed and there were celebrations in Britain as the troops came home. The war was to prove the catalyst for huge change in Argentina, for the fall of the junta created a vacuum in which the movement for democracy became irresistible. In October of 1983 the country returned to democracy, electing as President Raul Alfonsin, who had been a fierce critic of the junta's Falklands invasion. But Argentina has never dropped its claim to the Falklands and relations between the two countries, though vastly improved, are unlikely to be more than cordial until the sovereignty issue is sorted out.

Margaret Thatcher emerged rather better from the war than General Galtieri. Thatcher's popularity in Britain had sunk to a fairly low ebb before the Falklands campaign but, as was apparent on the night of the Argentine surrender, it soared afterwards. Political cartoonists were falling over each other to portray her, with perhaps grudging admiration, as everything from a female Winston Churchill to the new Boadicea. In June of 1983 Thatcher's Conservative Party won a second term in office, winning the general election in a landslide with a House of Commons majority of 144, much larger than anything since the Labour landslide of 1945.

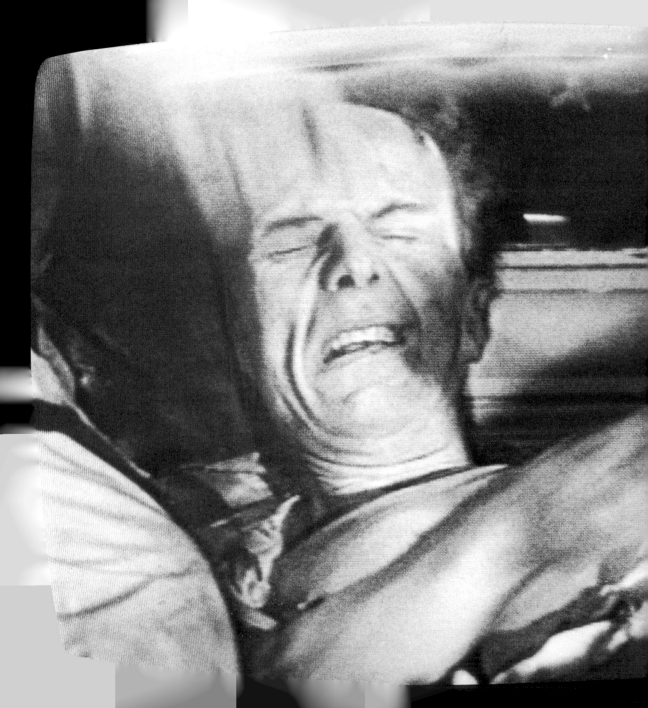

The Brighton Bombing 1984

Thatcher yards from death as IRA bombs Tory conference hotel

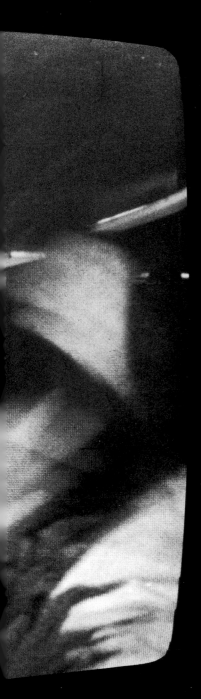

Norman Tebbit, seriously injured and in great pain, is placed in an ambulance.

THE GRAND HOTEL AT BRIGHTON during the Conservative Party conference of October 1984 rarely slept, but by 2.45 on the morning of 12 October it was about as quiet as it was likely to get. A couple of night staff were in the lobby, there was a certain amount of noise coming from the bar, where a few Tories and journalists had gathered, still in dinner suits, having just returned from the conference ball. Watchful security men were on patrol, inside and outside the building. Margaret Thatcher, the Prime Minister and Tory party leader, was, even at that late hour, among the few people in the hotel who were still awake. Thatcher, reputedly able to get by on three hours sleep a night, was sitting at a desk in her suite, checking over some papers in the red boxes that accompany politicians everywhere they go. Her husband, Denis, was in bed. At 2.54 a.m., the silence was broken by a tremendous explosion. A bathroom that Thatcher had been in a few minutes earlier was wrecked. The windows in her suite were blown out. There was a great gash in the front centre of the building, where the full force of the bomb had smashed through masonry and destroyed most of the two top floors.

Most of the British cabinet was in the hotel at the time. It was an IRA bomb and Thatcher and her ministers were quite clearly the target. The attack was the most direct ever launched against the British government. A few hours after the explosion, the IRA issued a statement that was as true as it was chilling: 'Today you have been lucky. But remember, you have to be lucky all the time, we only have to be lucky once.' There were five deaths and many injuries. Shocked television viewers, switching on the breakfast news programmes three hours after the explosion, saw Norman Tebbit, clearly seriously injured and in great pain, being carried from the wreckage on a stretcher. Tebbit, the Secretary of State for Industry, was to recover but his wife suffered even worse injuries and would be confined to a wheelchair. The wife of the Chief Whip, John Wakeham, died in the blast as did Sir Anthony Berry, a Conservative Member of Parliament.

John Timpson was presenting Radio 4's *Today* programme from Brighton during the conference. He gave listeners a graphic description of what had happened: 'I was in my room in the Metropole Hotel next door when the explosion woke me. When I got outside guests from the Grand were assembling on the promenade in front of the hotel. Some, like the Health Secretary Norman Fowler, had been in bed. He told me that he woke to the sound of crashing debris inside the hotel and joined a crocodile of guests who were filing down the main staircase through a cloud of dust and smoke. Others came down fire escapes, some, like the Education Secretary, Sir Keith Joseph, in dressing gowns and pyjamas. Others were in dinner jackets, they'd been to the conference ball and were in the hotel bar when the explosion happened: that too was extensively damaged. Rows of deckchairs were set up on the pavement for those badly shaken while ambulances took other casualties away…'.

Thatcher had gone to Brighton police station, outside which she was interviewed by a group of reporters including the BBC's then political editor, John Cole, who asked her how she was feeling: 'Very well, thank you very much. Our worry is whether there's anyone under that rubble. Geoffrey Howe (the Foreign Secretary) is here with us and Leon (Brittan, the Home Secretary) is here with us. We were all very, very fortunate. I was up working, I turned to do one final paper and then it went off. We were very lucky… We're anxiously awaiting news of other people. You hear about these atrocities, these bombs, you don't expect them to happen to you, but life must go on as usual. The conference will go on, as usual.' Thatcher repeated this last sentence, louder: 'The conference will go on, as usual'.

The conference did indeed go on, as did Britain's seemingly endless battle to solve the 'Irish question'. Its history goes back hundreds of years and even in this century involves countless decisions, treaties, initiatives, agreements, breakthroughs, false dawns, not to mention a hundred personalities who have come to the problem with high hopes and retreated sometime later, older, wiser but no closer to a solution. The issue, of course, is relatively simple: Ireland is an island divided in two, with the south an independent republic and the six counties of the north being part of the United Kingdom. The north is overwhelmingly Protestant, the republic overwhelmingly Roman Catholic. The Unionists, or Loyalists, of the north wish, on the whole, to remain part of the UK, while the Nationalists, who are mostly Catholic, would prefer to see Ireland reunified.

Northern Ireland was run by a devolved government (as opposed to direct rule from Westminster) the fact that there was an in-built Loyalist majority tended to lead to discrimination against Catholics. This could not excuse violence, but it did provide an excuse for violence.

The violence, when considered as a whole, was on an extraordinary scale and yet it had little impact on the British public's thinking about Ireland. Opinion polls throughout the time from 1969 to the present have shown that the British are resolutely indifferent to the Irish problem. Rarely do more than 5 per cent of them cite Ireland when asked what they regard as the most important issue facing the nation. This figure does not increase when the terrorists bring their campaign to the mainland, which they did with considerable frequency in the 1970s and 1980s. Between 1973, when the IRA bombed the Old Bailey, killing a caretaker, and 1996, when two people died in an explosion at Canary Wharf in the London Docklands, nearly 50 people died and more than 1,200 were injured in Irish Republican attacks on London alone.

In modern times, the Irish Republican Army and its political wing, Sinn Fein, pursued their unification ambitions via a mixed policy, usually described as a combination of 'the armalite and the ballot box'. This approach is in itself offensive to many Loyalists, who feel that they are being required to give ground and that if they do not they will be bombed. But there are extremists on both sides, Loyalist paramilitaries as well as Nationalist ones. There is a widespread acceptance that during the years when

The British Army had moved into Northern Ireland in 1969, following increasing amounts of street violence, notably a riot at Londonderry the year before. At first it seemed likely that the

(Left) The gutted upper storeys of the Grand Hotel after the IRA bomb exploded. (Right) The wrecked bathroom in which Mrs Thatcher had been a few minutes before the blast.

soldiers' main task would be to protect the Catholic population, which, in West Belfast, was coming under attack from Protestants. Indeed at that time the IRA's stock was low among Catholics. When the British arrived, local people took to describing the IRA as 'I Ran Away'. There has never been any reliable, publicized, estimate of the actual strength of the IRA, but it has never been thought to number more than a few hundred active personnel. Unfortunately it has been demonstrated all over the world that small terrorist groups can cause damage out of all proportion to their numerical strength and Thatcher was to see proof of that from the moment she came to power in 1979.

That year, three terrorist attacks brought home to the British government the scale of the problem it faced in Northern Ireland. In March, a few weeks before Thatcher won the May general election, a car bomb exploded in the underground car park at the House of Commons, killing Airey Neave, a Tory spokesman on Northern Ireland and one of Thatcher's closest friends and advisers. That bomb had been planted by the Irish National Liberation Army (INLA). It was an important moment, for Neave was the leading proponent of stricter security measures in Northern Ireland. He had also written the Tory manifesto for the coming election, which called for the establishment of regional councils in Northern Ireland.

The same year, at Warrenpoint in County Down, 18 British soldiers died when a bomb exploded and, on the same day, Lord

Mountbatten of Burma was killed by a bomb planted on his boat. There seemed to be no pattern to these bombings, nor was it clear why attacks on mainland targets would start and just as suddenly stop. Sometimes the bombs appeared to be in response to particular political initiatives, sometimes not. Nor was there much of a pattern in terms of the targets. In 1996 the *Daily Telegraph* analysed Home Office figures for bomb attacks carried out in London since 1973. There were 211 attacks all told, nearly all involving explosives although three people died and 14 were injured in shootings. Almost half the attacks involved shops, tourist attractions and pubs or restaurants. Military, political or judicial targets accounted for 47 attacks, 29 were economic targets and the rest involved transport or post offices. What the analysis proved was that no one was safe from the terrorists.

By the time of the Brighton bomb, security around Thatcher and the rest of the cabinet was tightening.

Many senior officers in the anti-terrorist squad believed that an attack on Thatcher was likely. The mainland campaign relented for several years after the death of Neave, but in 1982 the bombers were back in London, planting two devices in Royal parks which killed 11 people and injured 50. In 1983 a bomb outside Harrods in Kensington killed six people.

None of these attacks reduced Thatcher's resolve, for she regarded terrorism as one of the world's worst evils and the more there was of it the more she hated it. In many ways Thatcher's attitude to the Irish problem pretty much paralleled that of the average British person. Thatcher believed strongly in the union and had been known to point out, forcibly, that she was after all leader of the Conservative *and Unionist* Party. She came from a Protestant background in Grantham, and an active, practising Protestant background at that. There was little indication that she knew much about how it felt to be part of the minority Catholic population in a place like Northern Ireland.

If the issue did not emotionally engage Thatcher, her intellectual commitment was not in any doubt, even if Northern Ireland was hardly near the top of her priority list. In the early 1980s the Government decided to take a new route to a solution, namely via Dublin. This was a major change of policy, because until then the London approach had been unilateral, a policy of containment: Northern Ireland was a British problem which would require a wholly British solution. Now Thatcher opened a door to the Dublin government of Charles Haughey and the two leaders met three times between May 1980 and November 1981. This culminated in the establishment of the British-Irish Inter-Governmental Conference and that in turn led to the Anglo-Irish Agreement, signed by Thatcher in March 1985. The involvement of Dublin was important because Thatcher

believed, above all else, that it was essential to seal Northern Ireland's border with the south and that would be impossible without Dublin taking its share of the responsibility. The border area was rambling and mostly rural, making it impossible for the British to police on their own. Terrorist units based in the south had a relatively easy time crossing and criss-crossing the border, from their safe houses and bomb factories in the south to their targets in the north. Thatcher wanted that stopped.

After the Brighton bomb, the government continued to pursue a mixture of tough security measures in Northern Ireland combined with the continuation of the dialogue with Dublin through the new Anglo-Irish Agreement. Neither prong of the policy did much to stem the flow of bullets and semtex explosive into the hands of terrorists, who

were raising money for arms via their usual channels: bank raids, drug dealing and fund-raising in the United States. Over the years a sizeable number of people who settled in the US who came from Irish stock had acquired a somewhat romanticized notion of what the Irish 'struggle' was all about, assisted by politicians such as Senator Edward Kennedy. Indeed American visitors to 'the old country' were constantly surprised to discover that, in most of the Irish Republic, the IRA was regarded with a mixture of distaste and disdain. In the North, Sinn Fein candidates in local elections rarely attracted more than a third of the Catholic vote. Most Catholics vote for the Social Democratic and Labour Party (SDLP), led by John Hume.

After Brighton there was a succession of bombings that brought the level of public anger

**The Armistice Day
bombing at Enniskillen
was one of the worst
outrages of the entire
terrorist campaign.**

November:'The Government will
now intensify its efforts to find a basis
for the constitutional parties in
Northern Ireland to carry forward
the talks process… we are
determined to do all we can to bring
peace… the further killings over the
weekend make that search for peace
all the more urgent.'

Major's words tended to underpin
the belief in some circles that,
however much politicians deplored
the use of violence and claimed that
they would not be influenced by it,
there was a pattern that suggested
that bombs did influence policy. But
Major was determined to press on
with the political process. In
December 1993 the British and Irish
Governments signed the Downing
Street Declaration, which contained a vital, if
tacit, admission: that whatever might be thought
of the means, the aims of the two communities
in Northern Ireland were equally legitimate.
The Declaration said that if there was to be a
change in the constitutional structure of
Northern Ireland, this could only happen with
the consent of the Protestant and Catholic
communities. The reaction of the IRA was swift.
It decided that violence had, at least for the
time being, got it as far as it could go. The IRA
declared a ceasefire on 31 August 1994.
Loyalist paramilitaries followed suit in October.

There were no illusions in political circles as
to what this ceasefire meant, which was just as
well. Some argued that the paramilitaries had

about terrorism to new heights. In 1987, 11
people were killed during a Remembrance
Sunday service at Enniskillen, one of the worst
outrages of the entire terrorist campaign. Two
years later, a bomb at the Royal Marines Music
School in Deal, Kent, killed another 11. In 1992,
terrorists planted a bomb outside the Baltic
Exchange in the City of London; three people
died. There were two mainland bombings in
1993: one in Bishopsgate, London, killed one
person and injured 44. The other bombing, at
Warrington in Lancashire, killed two children.
By now John Major was Prime Minister and he
had begun a fresh round of efforts to build co-
operation through Dublin. The 1993 bombings
led him to tell the House of Commons in

actually come to the conclusion that they could only progress through talks. Others said that they were merely pausing, to regroup and bring in more arms. Ordinary people expressed the less sophisticated but nonetheless heartfelt view that they couldn't care less why the bombers had stopped, as long as they had. The political process continued, in Dublin, Belfast and London, only to be rudely interrupted in 1996 when the IRA bombed the London Docklands, killing two people, and the centre of Manchester, injuring more than 200. There was never any clear idea as to why these attacks occurred and there were rumours that they had been carried out by an IRA fringe hardline group that was opposed to the ceasefire.

Whatever had happened, the two 1996 attacks seemed to be aberrant. In 1997 the IRA once more declared a ceasefire and the impetus for political progress increased with the arrival of a new Labour government in London under Tony Blair. There followed an intense spell of negotiation, involving visits to Dublin and Belfast by Blair and trips to 10 Downing Street by all the Ulster political leaders, including Gerry Adams, the President of Sinn Fein. An agreement signed on Good Friday, 1998, formalized plans for an assembly in which all the parties who won seats agreed to sit. But the violence was not yet over, for in addition to the punishment shootings for which Irish paramilitaries continued to be infamous, there was a shocking bomb attack at Omagh on 15 August 1998. Twenty-eight people died, including children aged 18 months, 20 months, 8 years and 12 years, plus several teenagers,

people in their eighties and two people who were visiting the area from Spain. The casualty list served as an indictment of the entire terror campaign, demonstrating as it did that the real victims of these atrocities were not political structures or ideologies but ordinary people trying to live decent lives. The fact that the bomb had not been planted by any of the mainstream terrorist groups did nothing to assuage the feelings of horror, anger and grief that were apparent throughout the UK.

Yet the peace process survived, fragile as it was. As the century neared its end, politicians from all sides found themselves able to sit down in the same room and talk to each other. Anywhere else, this would have been a first step. In Northern Ireland, it had taken years and was a development worthy of limited rejoicing. There was no evidence that politicians from the Loyalist and Nationalist sides had actually gone so far as to shake hands, certainly not in public, but getting them inside the same four walls could be viewed as a step that would have been unthinkable even five years earlier. It was still too early to say whether fundamental attitudes, in Northern Ireland and towards Northern Ireland, had really changed. But there were some tentative reasons to think that the situation had at least moved on from 1970, the year after the modern Troubles began, when the then British Home Secretary, Reginald Maudling, visited the province to make an assessment of the situation. He was clearly not very impressed. 'For God's sake bring me a large Scotch' he said to an official. 'What a bloody awful country!'

The Lockerbie Disaster 1988

Ten-year hunt for justice after bombed airliner falls on Scottish town

The nose section of the Pan Am jumbo, Flight 103, lying on a hillside three miles from Lockerbie.

PAN AM FLIGHT 103 TOOK OFF FROM London's Heathrow airport at 6.25 p.m. on Wednesday 21 December 1988. There were 258 passengers and crew on board and much of their luggage was brightly wrapped, consisting of Christmas presents for friends and relatives in the United States. The passengers were the usual mix, found on more or less any international flight. They included 38 students from Syracuse University, the United Nations Commissioner for Namibia, an executive with the Associated Press, a senior vice-president with the American arm of Volkswagen. As the Boeing 747 lifted off the runway, people in the small Scottish market town of Lockerbie, about 275 miles from Heathrow, were sitting down for their evening meal or settling in front of the television or strolling to one of the local pubs for a pre-Christmas drink. Flight 103 climbed to a cruising height of 31,000 feet and the crew settled down for the transatlantic flight to New York, the next stopping place, although the flight's eventual destination was Detroit, Michigan. After a few minutes the aircraft's crew made contact with Scottish air traffic controllers. It was a routine call. There was no indication of any problem. Then, at 7.15 p.m., Flight 103 disappeared from air traffic control's radar screens.

In Lockerbie, Sam Anderson was inside his house when he heard a low rumble. Anderson, a 46-year-old driver of petrol tankers, went outside. 'There was a white flash, then an orange flash,' he said. 'I ran to the back of the house and saw hot orange fragments dropping, like from a volcano. It was devastating, really

The huge crater left by wreckage of the plane next to the A74 main road.

devastating, I've never seen anything like it.' Anderson lived about 100 yards from the main road that runs into Lockerbie. He saw that the road was covered with large chunks of masonry and what looked like floorboards and window frames. Anderson and others on the ground were already certain that an aircraft must have exploded, and it began to dawn on them that large parts of it had actually fallen on the town. The wreckage along the main road was the remains of houses that the aircraft had smashed into. A wing had fallen on to Sherwood Crescent, destroying half a dozen houses. Graham Byerley, who worked at a hotel near the main crash site, said: 'We initially heard a rumbling over the hotel, we thought the roof was coming in. Then we heard a tremendous shudder, as if there had been an earthquake. We saw sparks and an enormous ball of flame about 200 or 300 feet in the air. There was debris flying everywhere.' A caller to Independent Radio News, John Glasgow, said that he and others tried to get near the main wreckage of the aircraft, 'but it was completely on fire'. The nose section of the Boeing, largely intact, lay on its side on a hill three miles from the town centre. All 259 passengers on Flight 103, plus 11 people on the ground, were killed.

As is always the case with major accidents, various rumours spread quickly, including a story that two aircraft had collided. A massive mechanical failure was more likely and early reports centred on the age of the aircraft – it was an early 747 from 1970, but Boeing had extensively rebuilt it only a year before the accident. The last major 747 crash had been

three years earlier, in August 1985, when a
Japan Airlines Boeing crashed into a mountain,
killing 520 people.

It was quickly apparent at Lockerbie that
Flight 103 had exploded. While rescue teams
rushed to the scene, bringing ambulances, fire
engines, specialist cutting vehicles and RAF
search and rescue helicopters, Pan Am officials
and the British aviation authorities quickly
conferred. The wreckage was spread over a
large area, some 15 square miles, which clearly
indicated a very large explosion. The absence of
a Mayday call from the crew, which would have
almost certainly been received had the aircraft
suffered an internal mechanical failure, pointed
to a very sudden and massive explosion.

Experts assembled at the site soon reached
the conclusion that Flight 103 had been
destroyed by a bomb. They were right. The
long, painstaking examination of the wreckage
that followed the crash produced a Toshiba
tape recorder, inside which were tell-tale signs
of explosive. The bomb had been packed inside
the tape recorder. Later, as investigators
worked to piece together the history of the
flight, they carried out forensic examination of
clothes in the suitcase containing the bomb.
These turned out to have been purchased
in Malta. That and other evidence brought
investigators to the conclusion that the case
containing the bomb had been placed aboard
an Air Malta flight from Luqa to Frankfurt,

One of the many
homes destroyed
as wreckage fell
on Lockerbie.

Germany (where Flight 103 originated) and transferred to the jumbo jet there. This meant that the bomb was already on the aircraft when it reached Heathrow.

The Lockerbie crash would have been tragic enough at any time; just before Christmas it carried a special poignancy. Only nine days earlier, there had been another major accident when a train ran into the back of another at Clapham, south-west London, killing more than 30 people. Now came Lockerbie, on a scale that eclipsed even Clapham. More than 190 Americans died aboard the Pan Am jet and that meant that British investigators, from the police, the security services and the Air Accident Investigation Board, were augmented, within hours of the crash, by officers from the Federal Bureau of Investigation (FBI) who flew into Britain on the morning after the crash. Within a day or two it became clear that Lockerbie was unlike many other such disasters in that its perpetrators would be rigorously pursued for many years, culminating in a trial that is expected to start shortly after this book is published. It was not generally known at the time, but has become clear since, that investigators already had some idea as to who might have planted the bomb.

International terrorism had been a blight on the 1970s and 1980s, with aircraft hijackings, bombs, hostage taking and other manifestations of a modern curse. In the case of Lockerbie, Libya and its leader, Colonel Gaddafi, were early on the list of suspects. The reason for that goes back to July 1988 when the American warship USS *Vincennes* accidentally fired a rocket at a civilian Iranian Airbus over the Gulf, killing everyone on the flight.

Ali-Akbar Mohteshemi, Iran's Interior Minister, went on television to say that the American 'crime' would be punished. There would be 'blood-spattered skies', he said. American intelligence subsequently claimed that Iran had paid $10 million to Amed Jibril, leader of one of the most violent Palestinian terrorist organizations, to blow up an American airliner.

Two months before Lockerbie, the German police raided addresses in Frankfurt and Dusseldorf, arresting 15 suspected terrorists. Among those held were Hafez Dalkamoni,

Abdullah Gandafar and Marwan Khreesat. In the boot of a car used by Dalkamoni the police found three Toshiba tape recorders. Each of them contained a bomb. The bombs each consisted of 1 lb of semtex explosive, the same type and the same amount that crash investigators estimated was used at Lockerbie. Some of the arrested men talked and several said that Khreesat had made five bombs in all. The other two were not found and investigators later came to the conclusion that one of them must have been used to blow up Flight 103. Dalkamoni and Gandafar were subsequently tried in Germany and found guilty of terrorist offences, not including Lockerbie, but Khreesat was released a few days after being arrested.

British investigations after Lockerbie led to another link with Jibril's group. After the discovery of the Malta link, investigators flew to the Maltese capital and interviewed Tony Gauci, who worked in the shop where the clothes were bought. Gauci was shown photographs of various men and initially identified Abu Talb but Talb was subsequently eliminated from the list of suspects. More recently, Gauci has said that he believes Abdelbaset Al-Megrahi, a Libyan, bought the clothes.

The long investigation of Lockerbie has undoubtedly brought considerable frustration to the families of the victims, not least because, from their standpoint, promising avenues one minute have turned into apparent cul de sacs the next. The Ahmed Jibril group, for so long prime suspects as the originators, suddenly ceased to be in the frame. Observers of the Middle East have long thought that the reason has to do with the Gulf War, in which President Assad of Syria supported the Allies against Saddam Hussein. At that time, the Jibril group was based in Syria. Soon after the war, President Bush of the United States, commenting on progress in the Lockerbie investigation, said that President Assad had taken 'a bum rap' in being accused of complicity in the Lockerbie bombing. That was the end of the trail leading to Jibril's group; from then on, the full focus of the investigation fell on Libya.

In 1991, after a long series of hearings, an American Grand Jury handed down an indictment which said that two Libyans, the aforementioned Al-Megrahi and Khalifa Fhimah, 'did maliciously cause the deaths of 270 persons' by 'wilfully and unlawfully causing to be placed a destructive device and substance in and aboard Pan Am Flight 103'. Given that a trial is pending, it would not be appropriate to detail evidence here. In any event, the dominating battle of the seven years since that indictment was handed down has not been about evidence, it has been about bringing the two men to trial, given that Colonel Gaddafi

was pledged not to release them for trial in the West. On 15 April 1991, the United Nations voted to place an embargo on goods to and from Libya. This embargo was directly linked to the Lockerbie suspects; if the suspects were handed over, the sanctions would be lifted.

There were several false dawns, including an announcement by Libya on 29 September 1993, that it no longer objected to the two men being tried in Scotland but the decision would be left to the suspects. Not unexpectedly, no more was heard of that initiative. While diplomats and politicians on both sides pursued various compromise solutions, the Lockerbie families, led by the redoubtable Jim Swire, were keeping up the pressure. Swire lobbied in London and Tripoli, which he visited in March 1998, along with a Scottish law professor, in an attempt to find a way out of the impasse. Shortly afterwards, word came that British and American officials, who had insisted all along that the trial had to be held in Scotland – because that was where the crime was committed – were now willing to consider a trial in a neutral country. This was a small step in the direction of Gaddafi's

position, though the only neutral territory he was prepared to consider was 'any Muslim country in the world'. The reports of a changed Anglo-American attitude were confirmed by announcements in London and Washington on 24 July 1998. Officials of the two countries said they were now willing to consider a third country option and that the Netherlands was the preferred country. This proposal was put to the United Nations the following month, August, and the UN announced that it would lift sanctions against Libya if Gaddafi agreed to hand over the suspects for trial in Holland.

Gaddafi's agreement to a third country trial was conditional. If the men were convicted, he said, they would have to serve their sentence in Libya. This was unacceptable to Britain and America, who had said that serving a prison sentence in Scotland was 'non-negotiable'. However, the British and the Americans agreed that Libya could set up a special embassy in Edinburgh for the duration of the time the men were in prison. Late in 1998, Gaddafi agreed to meet the UN Secretary-General, Kofi Annan, in Libya. Annan arrived, but Gaddafi was said to be unavailable. Thus the game continued, with

Gaddafi's behaviour revealing a pattern: he agreed to the trial in principle, in order to keep in motion the question of raising sanctions, but put up minor legal obstacles, thus preventing the trial actually taking place.

The breakthrough came in the spring of 1999 and it was achieved by President Nelson Mandela of South Africa. On a visit to Tripoli, Mandela announced on 19 March that Colonel Gaddafi had agreed to hand over the two suspects by 6 April. There was understandable scepticism among some of the Lockerbie families but most people agreed that such a public declaration of intent, made by a powerful African leader who would not look kindly on any reneging by Gaddafi, was the most hopeful sign so far. So it proved. Camp Zeist, a disused Nato airbase some 20 miles south-east of Amsterdam, was temporarily declared to be Scottish soil for the purposes of the trial. At a ceremony in Tripoli, the two suspects were handed over to officials from the United Nations and flown to Valkenburg, the diplomatic airport near The Hague, on 5 April. There, the pair were formally arrested by the Dutch police and extradited into the care of the Scottish court authorities. The next step was an appearance before Graham Cox, the Sheriff-Principal of South Strathclyde, Dumfries and Galloway. After that the men were returned to the custody of Scottish officials at Camp Zeist to await a trial that was not expected to start for many months.

The preparation of Camp Zeist for the trial had cost about £750,000. The two Libyans were at first held in a bombproof underground cell, guarded by prison officers brought in from Scotland. Later they would be moved to a brick building with barred windows. A school building within the complex, last used by the children of American service families, was converted into a court and a gymnasium was equipped to hold the hundreds of journalists expected to cover the trial. Three Scottish judges, sitting without a jury, will hear the case. In addition to the physical requirements of the trial, various other needs have had to be accommodated. Muslim prayer mats and Hallal food were brought in for the defendants, Scotch whisky, potato cakes and traditional flat sausages were provided for their guards.

In this way did one of the most exhaustive investigations in criminal history reach a climax. The Lockerbie families, having spent ten years in an emotionally draining, often frustrating battle for compensation on two fronts — the compensation of justice and the monetary compensation of damages for their terrible loss — now stood on the

The garden of remembrance at Lockerbie was constructed as a permanent memorial to those who died on Flight 103.

threshold of success. The trial would answer some questions about international terrorism and it would doubtless leave many more unanswered, including the question of Gaddafi's precise role in sponsoring terrorism around the world. The best that could be hoped for from the trial was that it would allow the families of the victims to draw some sort of line under the horrific events of 21 December 1988.

The Berlin Wall Comes Down 1989

People power brings down Berlin Wall to end the Cold War

Take that: East German guards look down as a sledgehammer is taken to the symbol of communist repression.

THERE ARE LUMPS OF IT ON mantelpieces, there are chunks thrown, half forgotten, into cupboards. A man in Hamburg bought a couple of wheelbarrows full and built a rockery out of it. Some people managed to secure a piece that incorporated graffiti, words like 'freedom' and 'justice' hurriedly engraved in chalk or paint. Some people have paid considerable sums of money for even the smallest lumps of the Berlin Wall even though it was one of the ugliest pieces of architecture ever assembled. As a work of art it is probably worth a lot more when reduced to its constituent parts than it was during its life as a curtain between one culture and another. The Berlin Wall is everywhere and nowhere, yet until the dramatic events of 1989 it had been so familiar that few people even considered the possibility that its life might be finite.

But it was and the proof came on 9 November 1989. At 7.00 p.m., Gunther Schabowski, a member of East Germany's ruling politburo, gave a televised news conference. During it, he announced that East Germans would in future only need a pass that would be easy to obtain to travel to the West. This was incredible, but it was only the start. Almost immediately thousands of people flocked to the various checkpoints, most of them without any sort of travel pass. The border guards were caught, as it were, off guard. They had not received any instructions about letting people through. But by now the whole atmosphere had changed. There was still some fear, but that was outweighed by the sense, conveyed in an almost telepathic way through the tens of thousands who were now streaming to the border, that the regime no longer had the upper hand. That had now passed to the people and the people were not to be denied. At crossings such as Checkpoint Charlie, places that had gone into modern legend as the symbols of Communist repression, the guards simply stood back. They even smiled. Some put down their weapons and embraced ordinary citizens. A matter of minutes earlier, the guards had still been under orders to shoot anyone who put a foot across the border.

Word of the dramatic change in policy had crossed the border quickly, indeed West

(Left) Berlin was the symbol, but the barrier ran right around East Germany. These women were meeting through the wire between Germany and The Netherlands.

German television was giving the story uninterrupted coverage. As thousands streamed through the checkpoints, there were equal numbers of West Germans to greet them. Relatives who had not met for years fell into each other's arms. People were climbing on the wall. They had shovels and pickaxes and iron bars. The crowds ranged on the eastern side began to chant: 'Tear down the wall! Open the gates!' But the word most loudly and most emphatically chanted was *wahnsinn*. It means 'ecstasy'. It was an amazing scene – a great mass of cheering, shoving, smiling, laughing people. For a generation they had lived under the rules that obliged them to get official permission if they gathered in a party of more than eight people, on pain of a visit from the dreaded secret police, the Stasi. So there was something almost surreal about being able to gather in a group of 8,000, 80,000 – who knows how many? – without the authorities batting an eyelid. Those of us watching on television in Britain could scarcely believe what we were seeing. Later in the night, the Brandenburg Gate opened. This, one of

Germany's greatest structures, had for a generation been a symbol of division, of a country split in two by ideology.

Many Germans, from both East and West, simply stood before the gate, crying silently. No one can hope to know how many East Germans stayed in the West that night but most of them left. After all, they had jobs and homes and families. They had stood on the wall, they had gazed into the colourful, neon, gaudy metropolis that was West Berlin, a place that to East Germans had about it the image of a forbidden city. The East Germans went home because at that point there was not much else to do. The fear and intimidation they had lived under, many of them for all of their lives, had now been banished. True, the East German government was still in place. True, the structures of Communism were still in place. But now the psychology had changed utterly and forever. The toothpaste was out of the tube and there was no putting it back. The only possible outcome now was a reunified Germany under a democratic structure.

The wall had been constructed in 1961. The East Germans began to build it, without warning, in the early hours of 13 August. It is important to realize that whereas Berlin was divided more or less equally between the Western and Eastern powers after World War II, the whole of Berlin was in East Germany,

therefore West Berlin was a prosperous, democratic outpost in the Communist bloc, an island of freedom. For many people the wall constituted an admission that Communism had failed. It was unique in history, in that it was built to keep people in rather than keep them out. Officially, the East German regime said that the wall was designed to keep out Western spies. The Moscow Communist newspaper *Pravda* reported that the wall had been built at the request of the people of East Germany. The truth was that before the wall was constructed, East Germany had been leaking people: doctors, teachers, builders, academics, professionals of every kind fled the Communist East for the capitalist West.

As a barrier, the wall was only partially successful. It did not prevent people trying to cross into the West, indeed it was to provide some heroic stories as the years went by. Perhaps the most spectacular escape was in 1979, when two families from Thuringia took off in a hot air balloon and successfully landed in Bavaria a few hours later. Less sophisticated escapes involved people trying to smash through the wall in trucks with reinforced bars attached to the front. Others tried to climb over. Others again used pickaxes to dig holes in the wall. The last recorded attempt at escape before the wall came down was in February 1989, when a man called Martin Notev swam across the River Spree. He reached the other side but the crew of an East German patrol boat snatched him as he rested, exhausted, on the bank. There was a major diplomatic

incident over Notev's escape, with protests from the West, and Notev was eventually handed over to Western officials. The number of East Germans caught by their own border guards during escape attempts is not known but it runs to many thousands. Between 1961 and 1989, almost 200 people died after being shot by East German border guards, whose snipers operated from watchtowers high above the wall.

The lesson of the border's 28-year existence was that you could not impose an ideology by putting up a fence, but learning that lesson was to cost much heartache before the extraordinary, joyful moment when the sheer force of the people's will brought down the wall. The BBC's Ben Bradshaw filed a piece for Radio 4's *From Our Own Correspondent* in October 1989 that summed up the ultimate hopelessness of trying to make East Germany a state with its own identity. Bradshaw filed the report from the north Bavarian town of Hof, where trainloads of East Germans were arriving to cross the border into West Germany. This was the beginning of the end of the East German Communist state, and as news spread that the East German regime's controls were at last being relaxed (too late to save the regime), tens of thousands of people flocked to the railway station at Hof to greet, with cheering and applause, their East German compatriots. Bradshaw said: 'A concerted effort by its government to cultivate some kind of East German national consciousness failed. For most East Germans, their condition remained an artificial one. They did not compare their lives with those of the Poles, Czechoslovaks or Russians, but with their German cousins in the West; cousins who drove a BMW and took three foreign holidays a year in countries of their choice. Many of those leaving East Germany at the moment profess to be doing so for political reasons. There is no reason to doubt them. But for others the incentive is more basic.

One 40-year-old arriving in Hof told me: "I've been working my guts out for 20 years and what have I got to show for it – a Lada".

East Germany has survived by keeping its people in. It has been able to do so because it was part of a solid political and military bloc in a divided world, and in which its allies played ball. But in rapidly changing central Europe, they, Hungary and Poland, at least, are no longer willing to do so.'

The political seeds of the Berlin Wall's destruction were sown in Moscow with the arrival of Mikhail Gorbachev as leader of the Soviet Union in 1985. Gorbachev was a reformer. One of his more unlikely achievements is to have introduced two words to the Western lexicon: *glasnost* (openness) and *perestroika* (restructuring). Gorbachev was a breath of fresh air, at least as far as Western leaders were concerned. 'I can do business with this man,' Margaret Thatcher said after a meeting with Gorbachev at 10 Downing Street. Whether the Soviet people could do business with Gorbachev was another matter. His time in power was marked by policy lurches from right to left and back again, sometimes coming across as radical reformer, at other times seeming to drag his feet over fundamental decisions relating to economic reform. The one thing that became very clear was that once the cork in the bottle holding back reform started to loosen, there was no stopping it. And there was no telling how many people would be soaked in the process.

Gorbachev was 54 years old when he came to power, the youngest Soviet leader since Josef

Stalin, who died in 1953. Gorbachev made his mark early on, demanding the democratization of the Soviet Union and launching vehement attacks against the privileges enjoyed by Communist Party functionaries. But these very functionaries, powerful men in the Soviet satellite states who could not be brought down by mere words, were to frustrate Gorbachev. Calls for reform were all very well, but the Soviet economy was near meltdown, with a huge budget deficit and a near-worthless currency. The need for the Soviet Union to borrow large sums of money from the West meant that the United States and the other Western powers were in a powerful position to lean on Gorbachev in two areas: arms control and greater freedom in Eastern Europe. A key moment in the development of Eastern bloc reforms came when Gorbachev and President Ronald Reagan of the United States held a summit at Reykjavik, Iceland, in October 1987. Gorbachev brought a proposal for a

massive reduction in the number of missiles held by the two sides, a proposal flatly rejected by Reagan. But it was the clearest indication so far that Gorbachev desperately needed to reduce arms spending to save the Soviet economy.

It was against this background that Gorbachev went to East Berlin in October 1989 for the celebrations marking the fortieth anniversary of East Germany. The hard line regime of Erich Honecker was already in considerable trouble, with pressure for reform mounting. There had been street demonstrations in various parts of East Germany, demanding democracy and economic reform. The month before Gorbachev arrived, the Nikolai Church in Leipzig became the headquarters of the growing opposition movement, with thousands of demonstrators gathering at the church every Monday night. Leipzig was to be a key centre of the reform movement. Also in September, the first official opposition parties had been established in East

Hand of friendship: Helmut Kohl reaches up to shake hands with East Germans on the night the wall came down.

was starting to crumble when Hungary began to dismantle its chicken-wire border with Austria, allowing people through with minimal documentation. Tens of thousands of people took advantage of this liberalization. Hungary had a special place in the hearts of reformers; as far back as 1956, more than 1,000 Soviet tanks had rolled into Hungary to crush an uprising against the Communists.

More than 30 years later, it was obvious to Gorbachev that military power could no longer be used to put down uprisings, peaceful or otherwise. But Gorbachev was as worried as Honecker about events in Hungary and East Germany, thus the Soviet leader presented both his cautious side and his progressive side when he arrived in East Berlin for the anniversary celebrations. He told the East German people to be patient. He understood their desire for reforms, but he said that the right vehicle for the reforms was Honecker's Communist Party. However, in a quote that was to become something of an epitaph for the regime, Gorbachev warned Honecker that 'those who are late will be punished by life'. It was an irony of later developments that the same epitaph could well have been applied to Gorbachev.

When Gorbachev flew home to Moscow from his visit to East Berlin he may or may not have known that East Germany's fortieth

Germany. Honecker was slightly loosening the grip of the Communists, though at the same time his regime was attempting to persuade people that the reforms in the Soviet Union did not apply in East Germany which, according to Honecker's view, was operating in a different environment. To ordinary East Germans, it was not a very convincing argument. And the pressure for reform in East Germany was being fuelled by events elsewhere. Earlier in 1989, there had been the clearest sign so far that the Communist bloc anniversary would be its last. Honecker, who was 78 years old, must certainly have known that his days were numbered, and now the pressure on him to go, from outside and inside the regime, became irresistible. On 18 October, Honecker resigned, citing ill health, and was replaced by Egon Krenz. Nine days later, the government announced that there would be an amnesty for all refugees who had left the country that year. This minor concession only served to encourage the opposition. It was clear that Krenz was just another Communist leader, roughly in the Honecker mould, who mistakenly thought that protestors could be bought off with a few concessions. But the demonstrations in Leipzig continued and increased, as was the case elsewhere. On one occasion in early November, more than half a million people gathered in East Berlin to demand freedom of speech. The sheer size of this demonstration, and the fact that the security forces uncharacteristically seemed at a loss to know what to do about it, indicated that the Communist regime had but a short time left to live. November 9 marked the end of its effective life.

The Communists did their best to cling to power after the wall came down by trying to define how power would be disbursed in future. Hans Modrow, the new Prime Minister, promised democratic reform, free elections, a free media and even 'a closer relationship with the European Community…' This response only served to demonstrate that East Germany's leaders had lost touch with East Germany's people. The leaders were no longer trusted, if they ever had been, and 40 years of pent-up opposition now came to the surface. Posters appeared everywhere, saying 'We are one people'. There were still plenty in the East who believed in Socialism, plenty who felt that a reformed GDR could survive, but they were a minority. The majority wanted reunification. The only reform they wanted was an end to the German Democratic Republic.

They would get their wish and much faster than most people, inside or outside the two Germanys, had anticipated. On 28 November, Chancellor Helmut Kohl of West Germany put forward a 10-point plan for the creation of one Germany. Kohl knew that grabbing the initiative was vital. He was a strong and popular leader and he needed to take advantage of that. His 10-point plan was, if anything, regarded as too cautious by most people in the East and Kohl needed to speed up its implementation. He went to Moscow in February 1990, an historic meeting at which he secured Gorbachev's support for a united Germany. National elections to a single unified parliament were scheduled for the end of the year. A new constitution had to be put together and, just as important, a single currency had to be introduced. Talks between Eastern and Western leaders over the constitution proved difficult on several issues, ranging from abortion law (much more liberal in the East) to rights about the ownership of private property (non-existent in the East).

There was the issue of the new Germany's political position; in exchange for agreeing to a unified Germany, Gorbachev had insisted that

Keyhole to a better world? A West German youth smiles at a passing East German woman a few days after the Berlin Wall came down.

Germany remain neutral. This was unthinkable, both for most Germans and for the Western allies. A compromise was worked out whereby the new Germany would become a member of Nato, but would not allow Nato troops to be stationed in the eastern half of the country.

The West had an important role to play in German unification and a strategic interest in ensuring that the new Germany was very much part of the Western community. But above all, the West wanted Germany unified and out of Communist hands, the faster the better. That sentiment was expressed most clearly by the American Secretary of State, James Baker, who told a German newspaper: 'This is Germany's reunification; tell us when and how, we'll support it.' The 'when' was to be sooner rather than later. Kohl had produced economic union in July of 1990 and at midnight on 3 October, less than a year after rejoicing crowds had gone home carrying pieces of the Berlin Wall, the black, red and gold flag of the reunified Germany was hoisted in front of the Reichstag building in Berlin, watched by the best part of half a million people. Berlin would, in time, once again be the capital of Germany. The Brandenburg Gate would, once again, become a conduit for traffic moving freely between west and east. The first single German elections since World War II were held on 3 December, 1990 and Kohl became the first Chancellor of the reunited Germany. Not only was the Berlin Wall down, but the entire edifice that had been the Warsaw Pact now lay in ruins. Dangers and difficulties lay ahead, but the Cold War, which had lasted for almost 50 years, was over.

The Resignation of Margaret Thatcher 1990

Tory plotters end 11 years of rule by the 'iron lady'

Last exit: Mrs Thatcher after telling cabinet colleagues that she had decided to resign.

JOHN SERGEANT, THE BBC'S CHIEF political correspondent, was standing on a pavement outside the British embassy in Paris on the night of Tuesday 20 November 1990. He was speaking into a microphone, live, to BBC1 viewers. It was dark. Margaret Thatcher, the British Prime Minister, was inside the embassy, consulting with her advisers. The door of the embassy could be seen over Sergeant's right shoulder, but, obviously, he could not be looking at the door and talking to the nation at the same time. Sergeant, the BBC and millions of people watching desperately wanted Thatcher to emerge, for she was, rather suddenly, at the centre of a huge and extraordinary drama. At last the door did open and Thatcher came down the embassy steps. Sergeant swung round and thrust his microphone into the forest of such implements that now conveyed her words.

The scale of the sensation had been presaged when the result of the ballot for party leader was announced a little earlier. For most of the life of the Conservative Party, leaders had been chosen by nods and winks, dinners at

the Carlton Club and various other 'soundings'. The modern party had decided that it needed to be more democratic, but the procedure adopted was sufficiently arcane to ensure that a calculator was essential equipment when the result was announced. To win, Thatcher needed 50 per cent of the votes (of Conservative MPs) plus one, but she also had to have at least 15 per cent more votes than the person coming second. Thus it was that during an extended 6 p.m. news on Radio 4, James Naughtie broke into the scheduled running order: 'We have news from Westminster. Mrs Thatcher has beaten Mr Heseltine, but not by a sufficient margin to avoid a second ballot. Mrs Thatcher 204 votes, Mr Heseltine 152 votes, abstentions 16. That is a remarkable result – because it means that Michael Heseltine has prevented Mrs Thatcher from winning the leadership on the first ballot.'

Outside the Paris embassy, Thatcher was calm. She had received the result of the first ballot in a telephone call from London. She noted that she had not quite won by a sufficient majority to obviate the need for a

second ballot: 'I am naturally very pleased that I got more than half the parliamentary party and disappointed that's not quite enough to win on the first ballot, so I confirm it is my intention to let my name go forward for the second ballot.' The casual listener could easily have gained the impression that Thatcher's career had suffered some kind of technical hitch, a minor blip. The truth was that as Thatcher stood on that pavement, her time as Prime Minister was fast approaching its end. The challenge mounted to her leadership by Heseltine had dealt her a fatal injury.

The ballot outcome rendered irrelevant the purpose of Thatcher's trip to Paris so far as the media was concerned. Thatcher was in Paris for a meeting of the Conference on Security and Co-operation in Europe but not a word about that would make the newspapers the next day. The story now, as so often over the 11 years since she came to power, was Thatcher herself. The Paris meeting was relevant in one respect; had it not taken place, Thatcher would have spent the previous 24 hours in London, a vital extra day to lobby waverers in the party. If two Conservatives who voted against her had gone the other way, she would have won outright. Certainly Thatcher seemed to feel that the vote was as good as won when she left for Paris. She had told the BBC: 'I most earnestly believe that I shall be in No 10 Downing Street at the end of this week. What makes me so confident?

Michael Heseltine, whose challenge brought down Thatcher, was the centre of attention on the day she resigned.

I think I have a marvellous team working with me and I think that we are all optimistic.' That night she attended, with other European leaders, an evening of festivities at the Palace of Versailles. There have been reports that her true feelings about the leadership contest emerged when a fellow leader told her at Versailles that he was confident she would win the second ballot. Thatcher is said to have replied: 'No, it's all over'.

She returned to London the following morning, Wednesday, and met with the Tory party chairman, Kenneth Baker, the Leader of the House of Commons, John MacGregor and Timothy Renton, the Chief Whip. Westminster was by now a seething cauldron of rumours, plots and counter-plots. To the extent that any consensus could be discerned, Thatcher's Prime Ministership was holed below the waterline. There were many in the party, loyal Thatcherites, who felt that if she ran in a second ballot she could be humiliated. Also, there was a chance that Heseltine, a hated figure among Thatcher supporters, could win a second straight fight against Thatcher, therefore putting a pro-European from the left of the party in Downing Street. Thatcher feared that Heseltine would unravel everything she had achieved. Whereas if she withdrew from the battle and resigned, other candidates could be put forward in the second ballot

who would split the Heseltine vote and render him unelectable.

Later on Wednesday Thatcher met with each member of the cabinet individually. Most brought grim news: either they would not support her in a second ballot, or they would support her but did not think she would win. By Wednesday evening Thatcher must have been convinced that the party in Parliament (there was never any doubt that the party in the country supported her) felt she should go. Nominations for the second ballot would close at noon the following day, Thursday, so there was not much time. A few junior ministers came to see her on Wednesday night, urging her to stay and fight, but after they had left Thatcher talked with the one man who clearly had her interests unambiguously at heart: her husband, Denis. His overwhelming desire was to avoid seeing his wife humiliated and he advised her accordingly. At 9 a.m. the next morning Thatcher called the cabinet together and told them that she would cease to be Prime Minister and party leader as soon as a new leader had been elected. She is said to have become tearful and had to stop speaking for a few moments. After the meeting, Thatcher issued a statement: 'I have concluded that the unity of the party and prospects of victory in a general election would be better served if I stood down to enable cabinet colleagues to enter the ballot for the leadership'.

The country as a whole could fairly be described as in a state of shock. By the kindest of measures, for every person who liked Thatcher there was one who loathed her, but

perhaps the secret of the nation's shock lay in the fact that even those who loathed her nursed a secret admiration for her. She was impossible to ignore, she was only 5 feet 4 inches tall yet she was a giant on the political stage. She had been Britain's first woman Prime Minister, she had been in power for well over 11 years and she won three general elections with majorities of 43, 144 and 102 respectively, albeit assisted by the parlous state of the Labour Party during that era. She had never lost a vote of confidence in the Commons and grassroots Tories routinely gave her 10-minute standing ovations at the annual conference. She had worn with pride the label 'iron lady', she had made a virtue of intransigence ('the lady's not for turning'). Her demeanour had become so regal that when her first grandchild arrived in 1989 she used the royal 'we' to announce: 'We have become a grandmother'. She had taken on the might of the British trade unions and won. She had introduced a new concept, privatization, to the language of politics and made it a creed. She had railed against European federalists, albeit that she was the Prime Minister who signed the Single European Act in 1986. She had sat at a desk, working, at three o'clock in the morning when an IRA bomb blew the hotel she was staying in to smithereens; her *en suite* bathroom was wrecked, yet she was unhurt. She had galvanized American presidents in time of war, first courting President Ronald

Reagan's help at the time of the Falklands and then making sure President George Bush stood firm when Iraq invaded Kuwait in August 1990. Thatcher was visiting Bush at the time and Bush later recalled that Thatcher said to him: 'Remember, George, this is no time to go wobbly'. Indeed the fact that Thatcher had been deposed with the Gulf War going on made the timing of her departure all the more remarkable. So what brought it about?

Many reasons have been cited over the years since and a combination of all of them certainly contributed to the fall of Thatcher. It had all started to unravel in 1989, with bickering over the extent to which Britain should get involved in the European Monetary System (EMS). In the autumn of that year, Nigel Lawson, the Chancellor of the Exchequer, resigned because he felt that his position was being undermined by Alan Walters, an outside adviser to Thatcher and a fierce critic of both the EMS and of Lawson's policy of managing the currency by having the pound sterling shadow the German Deutschmark. The British economy was in a fragile state, and the Tories' position in the opinion polls, lagging well behind Labour, proved that, whatever complexities might be involved, the British people always hold the government responsible for a weak economy. At the end of 1989, Sir Anthony Meyer, a backbencher with no power base, mounted a challenge to Thatcher's leadership. It was an exercise to test the water; Thatcher won, with 60 MPs either opposing her or abstaining. It was a precursor of the storm to come.

One of the black clouds in that storm was the poll tax. The Tories had pledged themselves to the reform of local government financing and this reform centred on abolishing the rates, the system under which home owners paid a tax to fund local spending. The tax was based on the value of their property. The system was undoubtedly flawed (people in rented property paid nothing, except indirectly) but it had lasted for a long time without many people complaining about it. The new system, the community charge or poll tax, had been implemented in Scotland in 1989 and was due for implementation in England and Wales in 1990. The rates had been paid per property; the community charge was a per head tax. It was to prove both unfair and largely uncollectable. It was based on the electoral register, so that people wishing to avoid paying the poll tax simply disappeared from the

register. The scale and intensity of opposition to the poll tax took the government by surprise. There were street riots, the worst of them occurring in central London when millions of pounds worth of damage was done to property and riot police had to be called in to clear the streets.

These and other matters conspired to put Thatcher in a vulnerable position. But who would challenge her? Michael Heseltine was perhaps the only person in the party for whom affection at the grass roots began to match that enjoyed by Thatcher. Heseltine had been in the cabinet until 1986, when he resigned during a row over whether the Westland helicopter firm should merge with a European or an American company. Heseltine, tall and with a mass of swept-back blonde hair, was a wealthy publisher. He spent the four years between 1986 and 1990 assiduously cultivating the Conservative Party around the country, touring the so-called rubber chicken circuit. He was the darling of the annual conference, rousing the membership with rhetorical flourishes that had them cheering him to the echo. Thatcher, by all accounts, loathed and mistrusted him. She felt, among other things, that he was soft on Europe.

The question for Heseltine was finding the right moment for his challenge. In this he had assistance: Sir Geoffrey Howe, the Deputy Prime Minister and Leader of the House of Commons, found the moment for him. Howe had been uncomfortable for some time with the stridency of Thatcher's anti-European rhetoric. On 30 October 1990, Thatcher made

Mrs Thatcher faces
the world's media
on the day her
Prime Ministership
effectively ended.

a statement to the House of Commons about the European Union summit in Rome, from which she had just returned. The continental members of the EU were moving ever closer to a single currency, with varying degrees of enthusiasm, but there was little enthusiasm in Britain, certainly not among the Thatcherites. The Rome summit had produced an agreement that the 'hard Ecu', basically a single currency for business transactions, could one day evolve into a general single currency, if that was the will of the people and governments in the member states. Thatcher reported this to the Commons. But during questions from MPs, her true feelings on the Ecu and various other European matters hardened. The European Commission, she said, wanted to 'extinguish democracy'. She would ensure that nobody created a federated Europe 'by the back door'.

She listed three ambitions beloved of Jacques Delors, then the President of the Commission and the *bête noir* of Europhobic Tories, dismissing each with the cry: 'No! No! No!'.

Thatcher was in her finest combative mood. But in the end her assault on Europe was to be the trigger for her demise.

Howe had been appalled by Thatcher's attitude to Europe for some years, but this was the last straw. Howe resigned on 1 November. He took his resignation letter to Thatcher and sat quietly in her office while she read it. The letter said that Howe was not a federalist, but that Thatcher's approach would make it harder for Britain to influence the debate in Europe. But the letter was as nothing compared with the resignation speech he made to the House of Commons on 13 November. Howe had said nothing in public over the days since his resignation, but his speech more than made up for that. The Labour politician Denis Healey once remarked that being criticized by Geoffrey Howe was 'like being savaged by a dead sheep', but that was in 1978. By 1990, Howe, although a mild, thoughtful and quietly spoken man, had clearly acquired some powers of savagery. The fact that each word he uttered seemed to have first been taken out of his mouth and examined under every light before being put back and delivered only made the impact of the speech he made now, to a packed and hushed Commons, all the greater. It was to be one of the greatest set-piece occasions in the modern history of the House of Commons.

Howe said that by presenting the nation with a stark choice between the sovereign state and European federalism, Thatcher was offering 'a false antithesis, a bogus dilemma'. He spoke of 'the nightmare image sometimes

conjured up by the Prime Minister, who sometimes seems to look out on a continent that is positively teeming with ill-intentioned people scheming, in her words, "to extinguish democracy, to dissolve our national identity'". Howe said that Thatcher was putting at risk 'the future of the nation'. Howe believed that government was about persuasion, but that within the Thatcher government this was now 'futile'. Howe spoke of his loyalty and the conflict between loyalty to the Prime Minister and loyalty to the nation. His last sentence was an invitation to challenge the Thatcher leadership: 'The time has come for others to consider their own response to the tragic conflict of loyalties with which I have myself wrestled for perhaps too long'. Thatcher sat

on the government front bench throughout the speech, showing little outward sign of what she must have been thinking or feeling. The next day, Wednesday 14 November, Heseltine announced that he would stand for the leadership.

After Thatcher announced that she would resign, the second round of balloting involved Heseltine, John Major and Douglas Hurd. Major was Thatcher's own choice for leader. She had promoted him rapidly – he first appeared in government only in 1986 – and he was appointed successively Chief Secretary to the Treasury, Foreign Secretary and Chancellor of the Exchequer, the post he held when he stood for the leadership. Major, who came from a working-class background in Brixton, south

London, led in the second round of voting, in spite of a potentially damaging remark by Thatcher, who said she would be a 'back seat driver'. Hurd and Heseltine withdrew, making a third ballot unnecessary. Major brought in Heseltine as Deputy Prime Minister and Heseltine was put in charge of getting rid of the poll tax, which he did in short order. There was much to do if Conservative electoral fortunes were to be restored. Through a combination of coming across as a new Government with fresh ideas plus the fact that the electorate remained unconvinced about Labour under Neil Kinnock, Major won the 1992 election, although with the Conservative majority reduced to 21.

The change of government proved to be more one of personality than of substance and, whatever divisions there had been beneath the surface in Thatcher's time, they now came

crashing through the permafrost under Major's less intimidating leadership. The poll tax was gone but Europe was to become an even more contentious issue, causing divisions in the Conservative Party that would be among the leading factors in its landslide defeat at the election in 1997. Thatcher had gone to the House of Lords as Baroness Thatcher, but her occasional appearances on television, usually railing against the horrors of Europe, brought wistful sighs from some of those watching. The impact of Thatcher on the population, as compared with Major's rather bland style, was perhaps best illustrated in a story told by Matthew Parris, the political sketch writer of *The Times*. Parris recalled meeting a group of junior hospital doctors, who explained that in checking whether a patient was concussed, they would ask a series of questions, including: who is the Prime Minister? During Thatcher's

(Left) Thatcher peeks out through an upstairs window as John Major arrives to become the new Prime Minister.

(Below) Margaret Thatcher holding back the tears as she is driven away from Downing Street with her husband.

time in Downing Street, the doctors found they had to drop this question because even people with concussion knew that Margaret Thatcher was Prime Minister. The doctors reinstated the question when Major took over, but then had to drop it again; they found that even people who were not concussed had never heard of John Major. The story may be apocryphal. The important thing is that Margaret Thatcher made it very easy to believe.

The Dunblane Massacre 1996

All the children who died under Hamilton's gunfire were in this primary school class.

SHORTLY AFTER 9 A.M. ON Wednesday, 13 March 1996, Diana Madill was broadcasting from the London studios of Radio 5 Live, talking with a correspondent in Israel. Suddenly Madill was handed a more urgent story from closer to home. 'Let me interrupt you just at this point,' Madill said, 'because I want to give out some news that is happening at home. Reports are coming in that one person is dead and several people have been injured after a shooting incident at Dunblane primary school in Scotland. We will bring you more news as soon as we get it... we know there are now a number of fatalities, according to the education authority in the area.'

This was to be the first report on a day when there would be many others, a day when nothing else would matter. Most British people were either at work or at school, or on their way to one or the other. I first heard the news when I switched on the television to check something on Ceefax but instead heard a news report on BBC1. There is news that is compelling and there is news that is horrifying. Occasionally there is news that is both and this was it. Soon it became clear that 15 children and one of their teachers had died immediately at Dunblane (another child would die later). Journalists are routinely described as 'hard-bitten' and most of the time that is part of the job, otherwise the job might not get done. But Dunblane was not a story that could be reported with the detachment of experience. At the time, and in researching this book, Dunblane stands out, for me, as a dreadful and wrenching story. The murder of children is in a

Slaughter of the innocents:
gunman slays children in Scottish school

category of its own, an occurrence that defies conventional logic. Thus Dunblane was perhaps worse, in its way, than the tragedy at Aberfan in October 1966, when a slag heap collapsed on to a school killing 116 children and 28 adults. The numbers were greater at Aberfan, but a tragedy is not measured in numbers. Somehow the wilful destruction of young life goes beyond anything else. And there is something especially distressing about the murder of children when it happens in their school, a place that parents hope to be able to regard as a sanctuary, a home away from home in which our children are given over to the care of teachers just as dedicated to their welfare as the parents themselves.

Dunblane in 1996 was, as it remains, a small town, perhaps no more than a large village; a

good place, to live in and to visit. Dunblane was a well-kept town, with elegant stone villas. Most of the people living there would regard themselves as successful, decent and hard working. There was a sense of community, everyone knew everyone else. Certainly nearly everyone knew Thomas Hamilton, who was a frequent visitor to the town from Stirling, 14 miles away, where he lived. There was something about Hamilton that the people of Dunblane did not like. He had been connected with youth clubs and scout troops in the town, but stories began to circulate about Hamilton that made parents mistrust him. This mistrust was extremely well founded but in Hamilton it was to become a focus for resentment. Hamilton would visit Dunblane again, for the last time, on the morning of 13 March.

Prime Minister John
Major and Labour
leader Tony Blair
visited the school
together soon after
the shootings.

At the beginning of the week, Hamilton had posted seven letters to various media outlets in Scotland, including the *Glasgow Herald*, Scottish Television and the newsdesk of the BBC in Glasgow. The letters, which included a copy of one he had sent to the Queen, detailed various grudges Hamilton had against the parents and teachers of Dunblane. He accused them of slander. He said that they had spread lies about him and the nature of his relationships with children in the area. These letters were sent carrying second-class stamps, so Hamilton must have known that they would not arrive at their destinations until Thursday. This may have meant nothing, or it may have meant that Hamilton wanted the media to have these letters on Thursday morning as a sort of explanation for what had happened the previous day.

On Tuesday, Hamilton rented a white van. He visited his mother that evening and the van spent the night parked outside Hamilton's grubby, untidy flat in Kent Road, Stirling. It was a cold night and a neighbour recalls a brief conversation with Hamilton outside in the street the following morning, where he was scraping ice from the windscreen of the van. The conversation was inconsequential and the neighbour said later that Hamilton did not seem unusually agitated. The conversation took place at 8.30 a.m. In Dunblane, 14 miles away, children were preparing for school. At 9 a.m., with the children already in school, Hamilton drove to Dunblane, parked the van and walked in through the school gates. He was carrying four weapons, one in each hand and two more

in his pockets. He walked to the back of the main building and crossed the playground, which was painted with a hopscotch grid. Hamilton turned, started walking towards the cloakroom and raised the guns. He fired. The first two or three bullets went through the windows of a prefabricated classroom. Andrea Knox, an 11-year-old who had been sent from the classroom to fetch something from another part of the building, glanced out of a window and saw Hamilton: 'He turned round and looked straight at me' she said later. So far, no one was hurt. Hamilton walked through the cloakroom and towards the gymnasium, where 27 children from the Primary 1 class were starting a physical education lesson. The children were five and six years old.

Hamilton walked into the gym, pulled out the two guns and started firing. When the need arose, he stopped to reload. It was all over in a few minutes. Hamilton had killed 15 children and their class teacher, Gwen Mayor. Another 11 children were injured, one of whom died later.

Hamilton was also dead, lying in a corner; when the mayhem was over, he shot himself through the head. The school's headmaster, Ron Taylor, ran into the gym after being alerted by the noise: 'It was an appalling mess' he said later. 'We did what we could. We tried to stem the blood, we just did what we could. But it was so little, so little'. John McEwan, leader of the paramedic team that arrived a few minutes after the shootings, came upon a scene of numbing tragedy. 'There were little bodies in piles dotted around the room and items of children's clothing, pumps and shoes, on the floor', he said in an interview with the *Sunday Times*.

'One boy of about five was sitting on the floor looking confused and shocked, pointing at a bullet hole in his arm. He obviously couldn't grasp what had happened. He was so shocked he couldn't cry. The gunman was lying in a corner. It was difficult not to feel loathing and disgust for the man.

For the first time in my life, I had this over-whelming desire to mutilate that corpse. I know that sounds terrible. I had to force myself not to kick him as I walked by.'

Dr Brenda Fleming, an accident and emergency consultant, arrived from Stirling Royal Infirmary. She went to each of the children to check for a pulse. For those who were wounded, she set up drips and oxygen supplies. Dr Fleming found three survivors in a cupboard, where they had run for safety when the shooting started. Dr Fleming said: 'As I walked in, the teacher who had died and a young girl were just at my feet to the right. The rest of the room was sprayed with bodies and it looked as though they had just died where they fell. It didn't look as though they survived long enough to move an arm or a leg. A lot of us still feel it was not real. If someone had walked into the gym and said, "this is Hollywood, stop filming" we would have believed them.'

News of the massacre spread like a shockwave across the nation. Michael Forsyth, Secretary of State for Scotland in the Conservative government, cancelled his London engagements for that day and flew to Dunblane, stopping only to collect his Labour opposite number, George Robertson. Both men had strong ties with the area: Forsyth was Dunblane's MP and Robertson actually lived in the town. Both men knew the school and many of the children and parents. The arrival of Forsyth and Robertson, together, signalled that some tragedies transcend politics, a message that was to be reinforced later when John Major, the Prime Minister, flew to Dunblane with Tony Blair, the Opposition leader at the time. There would be divisions between them over the gun control legislation that Dunblane provoked, but those differences were not, on the whole, along party lines.

Hardly had the nation absorbed what had happened before it was asking the question: why? There had been shooting outrages before,

notably when Michael Ryan ran amok at Hungerford, but the murder of children on this scale inside the supposed safety of their own school was without precedent. As the media investigated Hamilton, some of the answers were provided. Thomas Watt Hamilton was 43 years old when he murdered the children. His shooting prowess, all too amply demonstrated at the school, came from a long-standing interest in guns. Less than a month before the massacre, Hamilton had applied for membership at the Callander Rifle and Pistol Club, about 14 miles from Dunblane. He was allowed to demonstrate his skills on the club's range. The members were impressed with his ability with a 9mm pistol of the kind he was to use at Dunblane. He seemed intent on emptying a magazine of bullets as quickly as possible and it was noticed that he showed no interest in checking the target afterwards, which was extremely unusual. Several of the members

who used the range while Hamilton was there spoke of his 'intensity'. The club turned down his membership application. Hamilton had owned guns for at least 20 years and he held them legally. Scottish police were to be asked after the shootings why it was that his licence to hold firearms had been first granted and then renewed. The answer was that, under the laws in force at the time, there appeared to be no reason why Hamilton should be refused a licence. Indeed in some respects, Hamilton's suitability or otherwise to own weapons was a red herring. Guns are obtainable, legally or otherwise. It was the reason why Hamilton wanted guns, the reason why, in particular, he would turn them against children that was the core issue.

Hamilton had been brought up in a tough Glasgow neighbourhood. Money was tight and his parents split up when he was an infant; Hamilton's mother had him adopted by her

time, he had already become involved in the Scouting movement. He had been an assistant Scout leader for a year when, in 1974, he was sacked after complaints from parents. These complaints arose from a camping trip, during which Hamilton had made a group of boys sleep in the back of a van in freezing weather. After a second, similar trip, the Scouts returned to say that they had been forced to stay in soaking wet clothes and dig snow holes. Parents complained and Hamilton was thrown out of the Scouts, although he would write endless letters over the next decade and more trying to get reinstated.

As Hamilton could not be part of the Scout movement, he started his own boys' clubs. He opened at least a dozen, in Dunblane, Glasgow and elsewhere, many of them using the name 'Rover', a Scout term presumably designed to make parents think that he had some connection with the real Scouts. The pattern was similar in each case: the club would open, parents would send their children along, rumours would start about 'odd' behaviour by Hamilton, the children would be withdrawn from the club, the club would close, another would open. Hamilton appeared to have a fascination with Dunblane, where he started a number of these clubs, though no one quite knew why. The exact nature of Hamilton's misbehaviour was by now beginning to crystallize, though there was still no proof.

parents. They subsequently moved to Stirling, where Hamilton attended the Riverside secondary school. He was not much liked, either by the teachers or the other pupils. As an adolescent, Hamilton revealed a nasty streak. He would bully girls to get them to play with him. He seemed to have paranoid tendencies, constantly complaining that other pupils, and adults, were singling him out for criticism. He became morose and introspective, a loner. Hamilton was not very attentive in class and he left the Riverside without qualifications. His malicious behaviour was becoming bizarre by his late teens, with one former neighbour recalling that Hamilton used to telephone his mother and breathe heavily down the phone before hanging up.

By the 1970s Hamilton had begun on the path that was to end in the gymnasium at Dunblane School. Hamilton had opened a DIY shop in Stirling but the business failed. By that

It emerged that Hamilton had gone to a Boys' Brigade camp, after which there was talk of Hamilton having taken hundreds of photographs of boys in underpants or shorts. There were also stories circulating of Hamilton requiring the boys to show their chests as part of an 'inspection'.

The first formal complaints about Hamilton surfaced in 1983 when he was banned from running a boys' club that met on the premises of Dunblane High School. There had been 'serious allegations' made against him, all denied by Hamilton, who was so vehement in his denials that he complained to the local government ombudsman and won the case. Yet the evidence of wrongdoing against Hamilton was mounting, if circumstantial. Strathclyde Police were called in to investigate a specific set of complaints against him, including some relating to a camp at Loch Lomond in 1989 where Hamilton forced boys to run around in the

nude and made them rub suntan lotion on his body. One mother with a child involved in that case made a statement to police and handed over a number of photographs, but Hamilton was never prosecuted. The mother has said since that Hamilton threatened her with a gun.

At least one child was withdrawn from a camp that Hamilton ran when the child's mother discovered that Hamilton was taking videos of the boys while they were naked. The difficulty for the police was that Hamilton had not done anything that was against the law. He appeared to be a paedophile but no one could prove it. There was no evidence that he was active, in the sense that no one had complained of being touched. In 1994, the police raided Hamilton's flat in Stirling in connection with paedophile photographs, but nothing was found and no action was taken. Meanwhile Hamilton kept on opening boys' clubs, the latest one at Bishopbriggs, Glasgow, which met

only two nights before the Dunblane shootings. But Hamilton's resentment was clearly building to the point of rage, a rage that was focused on the people of Dunblane. With the benefit of hindsight, it could be seen that Hamilton was homing in on that town and on its primary school. In 1995, he distributed leaflets around the town, complaining about the allegations against him and saying that he had been obliged to stay off the streets to avoid 'embarrassing ridicule'. On 26 January, two months before the massacre, he wrote to education chiefs complaining that teachers at Dunblane primary

school had 'contaminated all of the older boys with this poison, even former cleaners and dinner ladies have been told by the teachers at the school (that) I am a pervert… all of this has been extremely damaging, not only to my clubs but to my public standing'.

Seen from the vantage point of what happened at Dunblane school, Hamilton was by now winding himself up for drastic action. Seen from any other viewpoint, his actions were simply the continuation of his campaign, the pursuit of his grievance. He wrote another letter in February complaining about the effect

(Left) Parents of the Dunblane victims gather to respond to government proposals on the curbing of handguns.

(Below) Michael Howard, Home Secretary, with guns handed in during an amnesty called after the Dunblane massacre.

the rumours were having on his clubs. He said that the number of boys from Dunblane attending his camps had fallen from 70 in 1983 to one in 1995. He also wrote to Michael Forsyth, along the same lines. On 7 March, he wrote to the Queen. By that time, a new gun had been sent to Hamilton at his flat in Stirling, seemingly by mail order. There were reports soon after the shootings that, two weeks before, Hamilton had been seen in the grounds of another primary school, in Stirling. The letters, the delivery of the gun, the school visit and other random events now coagulated, became part of a singular path towards a bloody denouement.

The only question remaining was why Hamilton had chosen to visit his resentment on children. If his grievance was about the behaviour of adults in condemning him as a danger to their children, why did he not take his revenge on adults – on the parents, or the police, or the education authority? Psychologists, for once in broad agreement, said that in seeking to look after children, through his clubs and camps, Hamilton was seeking the parents' acceptance. He was saying that he could be trusted, but his behaviour with the children meant that he could not be trusted. In Hamilton's mind, this had nothing to do with the children as such, it was the fault of the parents. And if there was

one sure and savage way to punish parents, it was to take away their children. That is what Hamilton thought he was doing on 13 March 1996. He took the lives of 16 children, in order to take revenge on their parents.

The Death of Diana, Princess of Wales 1997

Diana, the 'queen of people's hearts', killed in Paris car crash

Candles in the wind: one of the countless tributes to Diana.

I ONCE ASKED A DISTINGUISHED British magazine editor what subjects she would put on her cover if she wanted to boost circulation. 'Diana, sex or slimming…' she replied, '…in that order.' After a moment's pause she added: 'Come to think of it, there have been times when putting Diana's face on the cover allowed you to deal with all three subjects in one'. In the first week of September 1997, more than a hundred magazines in Britain and America alone, and countless more around the world, had on their covers a photograph of Diana, Princess of Wales. But the subject this time was not her sex appeal or her battles with slimming-related food disorders. The reason, in that momentous week, was that she was dead.

This, the last chapter in this book, deals with an event that will be more familiar to readers than any of the others. Wars, assassinations, moon landings and sundry disasters can fairly said to have been more significant and important in this century than the death of a princess. But significance and importance are not the only measures of a story. That is why I would nominate the death of Diana as the most stunning single news story of the century. If that seems like overstatement, a surrender to hype, I can only argue that Diana was, surely, the most famous woman in the world and that her death at the age of 36 was an extraordinary shock for hundreds of millions of people. Issues arose at the time to do with whether we really ought to be so focused on a single individual with no real power over our lives, a woman of privilege and wealth whose persona often seemed to be a creation of the media . But that is to tackle the reasons why Diana was famous. The fact that she was so famous is what made her death a stupendous event.

Diana had flown to Paris from the south of France with her boyfriend Dodi Al Fayed, son of the Harrods owner Mohamed Al Fayed, on the afternoon of Saturday, 30 August. They travelled in a private aircraft and landed at Le Bourget airport. Later they went to the Ritz Hotel, also owned by Dodi's father. They had at first planned to go out to dinner but then changed their minds and had something to eat in their hotel suite. Shortly after midnight, as 30

(Below) Dodi and
Diana pursued by
the paparazzi while
on holiday a few
days before the
fatal crash.

(Right) Police
teams with the
wrecked Mercedes
in the Paris
underpass soon
after the accident.

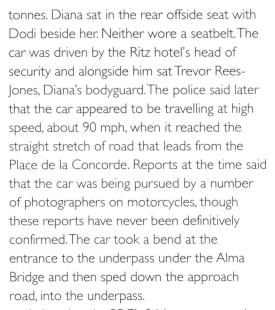

August turned into 31 August, they left the hotel, having apparently decided to go to Dodi's apartment on the other side of Paris. Hotel closed circuit footage shows them leaving the hotel, but not before elaborate arrangements had been made to try to mislead the photographers who followed Diana's every move. A fleet of cars, led by a Range Rover, drove away at high speed from the front of the hotel, pursued by some of the photographers. A visitor to Paris from London recalled later seeing the Range Rover drive away. He then saw a photographer on a motor cycle drive up and call out to other photographers: 'She's left by a side entrance, let's go.'

Diana had indeed left by a side entrance. She and Dodi got into the back of a black Mercedes, the largest limousine made by the German company and frequently used to carry heads of state. The car has a powerful six cylinder engine and weighs more than two

tonnes. Diana sat in the rear offside seat with Dodi beside her. Neither wore a seatbelt. The car was driven by the Ritz hotel's head of security and alongside him sat Trevor Rees-Jones, Diana's bodyguard. The police said later that the car appeared to be travelling at high speed, about 90 mph, when it reached the straight stretch of road that leads from the Place de la Concorde. Reports at the time said that the car was being pursued by a number of photographers on motorcycles, though these reports have never been definitively confirmed. The car took a bend at the entrance to the underpass under the Alma Bridge and then sped down the approach road, into the underpass.

In London the BBC's 24-hour news and sport network, Radio 5 Live, was transmitting *Up All Night*, a news and magazine programme mostly heard by insomniacs, lorry drivers and other night workers. At 2 a.m. Gail Downey read the news. She said that the princess had been involved in a car accident in Paris. Already it was known that Dodi Al Fayed was dead. The early reports were not in any way alarmist, indeed they gave rise to hope. There were unconfirmed reports from the scene that the princess had been seen outside the car and walking unaided. Next the reports said that the princess was in fact seriously hurt and had been taken to hospital. It was several hours before it was announced that the princess was dead.

Most people in Britain would have heard the news on their radio alarms as

they awoke that Sunday morning. The BBC merged four of its five national radio stations (the exception was Radio 1) and all its local radio stations into one continuous news service. Both BBC television networks covered the story continuously, as did ITV. Radio listeners awoke to a special edition of the *Today* programme, fronted by James Naughtie, one of the regular presenters, and Peter Allen, then co-presenter of the breakfast show on Radio 5 Live. They had plenty to report.

A British witness, Gary Dean from London, said he had seen the Mercedes enter the underpass at high speed, perhaps 100 mph. 'I thought to myself, this car is going too fast for safety. It hurtled past me. After it entered the tunnel I heard a crash followed by a series of thuds.'

Dean said that he did not see any motorcycles enter the underpass after the car, which had struck the side of the underpass and then bounced off, crashed into a pillar and come to rest. Such was the force that much of the engine had been driven backwards into the front passenger compartment, where the driver lay dead and Rees-Jones was seriously injured.

Paramedics and doctors spent a long time at the scene treating Diana and firemen had to cut the roof off the car to get the occupants out, which took 90 minutes. The firemen were still at work when news of who was in the car reached the French government, which immediately contacted the British embassy in Paris, which telephoned the Foreign Office. The Princess was taken to hospital, where a team of surgeons worked to save her life. The injuries were too severe. Bruno Riou, head of the intensive care unit, said later: 'Her chest cavity

was urgently opened up, revealing a significant wound to her left pulmonary vein. Despite a closure of the wound and an external and internal cardiac massage lasting two hours, no effective circulation could be re-established.' The princess was dead.

The fact that fantastic stories soon began circulating is of little importance now. Dodi and Diana were about to become engaged – no evidence for this claim exists. The crash was caused by the pursuing paparazzi – again, there is no evidence, although a number of photographers at the scene of the crash were questioned for several days. The British security services had murdered the couple, by shining a bright light in the driver's eyes, to prevent them marrying – a claim too fanciful to warrant further attention. A Fiat Uno car had caused the crash by swerving in front of the Mercedes – no such car was ever found. These and other theories were soon displaced by the news that the car's driver had more than the legal limit of alcohol in his blood, although that may only have been a factor when taken together with the speed of the car. The simple truth was that Diana had died in a car crash and, as with many

car crashes, it was unlikely that any one cause would ever be identified. Even the famous suffer inexplicable accidents.

There were some who thought that Diana's early demise was pre-ordained and in some senses that theory is attractive. In spite of the wealth and fame she achieved, the omens had not looked especially good in her early life as Lady Diana Spencer. For a start, she was the 'wrong' gender and she would sometimes laughingly refer to herself as 'the girl who was supposed to be a boy' . Her father, Viscount Althorp, later the eighth Earl Spencer, and his first wife, the Hon. Frances Roche, had two daughters before Diana was born and Viscount Althorp wanted a male heir. A son had been born in 1960 but he only lived for a few hours. Frances quickly became pregnant again but gave birth to another girl: Diana was born on 1 July 1961. Diana was only six years old when Lady Althorp left the family home, Park House in Norfolk, at the start of what was intended to be a trial separation, but the marriage never resumed and the couple were divorced in 1969. At roughly the same time as her mother left, Diana's two sisters went away to boarding school. So Diana was left alone with a feeling of betrayal: she felt that, as she put it later, she had been deserted.

Diana was educated in Norfolk and at boarding school in Kent, from which she emerged without any O-level passes. She worked variously as a nanny and a babysitter, and later at the Young England Kindergarten in Pimlico, London, during which time it became apparent that she had something more important than O-levels: compassion. This trait may have arisen from her childhood travails, which would have given her a particular feel for the position of children and others who are powerless to control their own fate. She was already a striking young woman when she first met the Prince of Wales, 'in a ploughed field' as both later recalled it, at Althorp, where the Prince was visiting Lady Sarah Spencer, Diana's elder sister. That was in 1977. The first public indication of a romance came three years later when a tabloid reporter was scanning the banks of the River Dee near Balmoral through a pair of binoculars: he spotted Diana with Prince Charles. From that day in the idyllic surroundings of Balmoral to the moment when she died in a Paris underpass, there was never a moment when Diana was out of the public eye.

The media, and especially the tabloid press, was in a sentimental frenzy at news of the royal romance. Diana was the girl next door. So ordinary! She lived in a flat with two other girls and shopped at Marks & Spencer! She was good looking! Such was the fairytale nature of the press coverage that no one bothered with

the warning signs: that Diana was still a teenager (though she turned 20 by the time of the wedding) and fully 12 years younger than Charles; that she was a fun-loving girl who enjoyed pop music, whereas Charles was a serious minded man with little interest in contemporary music; that Charles had never shown much interest in marriage but was known to have a relationship with a married woman, Camilla Parker Bowles. These matters could wait, as far as the press was concerned. The nation wanted a royal wedding and got one, on 29 July 1981 at St Paul's Cathedral. The great and the good gathered from far and wide, including President Reagan from the United States and the King of Tonga, for whom a special chair had to be built to accommodate his girth. Three orchestras played and Kiri Te Kanawa sang, all watched by the largest television audience in history.

How long would it be before the fairy tale turned sour? By one account it was only a matter of hours. The couple spent their wedding night at Broadlands, an estate in Hampshire, and it was noted that the prince rose very early the next morning to go fishing in the River Test. Diana had always come across as a believer in romantic love. If she had doubts she put them aside, just as she tried to put aside the prince's relationship with Mrs Parker Bowles, which she knew about. This was not a relationship Prince Charles had done much to hide. During the honeymoon, most of which took place aboard the royal yacht *Britannia* in the Mediterranean, there was one occasion when the prince arrived at the dinner table wearing a pair of cufflinks engraved 'CC' – a gift from Mrs Parker Bowles.

The couple's children, Prince William and Prince Harry, were born in 1982 and 1984 respectively and they undoubtedly provided Diana with the greatest fulfilment in her family life, the marriage itself having become increasingly cold and distant. The relationship turned into a soap opera, with each of the participants taking various steps to court public sympathy, by briefing sympathetic journalists. The most disastrous manifestations of this increasingly bitter battle were the two television interviews given, separately, by the prince and princess, in the course of which each admitted adultery. The more famous, or notorious, was the one given by Diana to Martin Bashir for BBC 1's *Panorama*, in which the princess said that she did not expect to be Queen of England but that she did hope to become 'the queen of people's hearts'. There was also Andrew Morton's book, *Diana: Her True Story*, which recounted tales of eating disorders and a suicide attempt. The couple's divorce, in August of 1996, had become inevitable.

Diana had long since thrown herself into charity work and it was in this area that many millions of people warmed to her. She may have proved good at stealing the limelight from Charles by appearing in sensational dresses and pausing just long enough to maximize the number of photographs taken, but she also knew how to commune with ordinary people. Her work for AIDS charities did more than anything else to raise public understanding of that disease. She was seen shaking hands with and embracing AIDS victims at a time when AIDS was still being touted as a 'gay plague' by some newspapers. Although Diana gave up much of her charity work in 1993 to give herself more time out of the limelight, she continued with AIDS charities and to pursue a campaign to get land mines banned, a campaign that led to an international treaty being agreed after her death. By the time of the Paris accident she was undoubtedly at the height of her public popularity and seemed to have found private happiness with Dodi.

The week between Diana's death and her funeral was one of the most extraordinary of modern times. The British nation seemed to plunge itself into an orgy of mourning, bringing forth endless newspaper articles and television programmes claiming that somehow Diana had broken through the permafrost of English reserve to uncover a country that could, after all, display its feelings in public. This always looked like an exaggerated response, but there is no doubting the outpouring of affection for Diana, beginning on the very night of her death when night-club disc jockeys in the West End of London announced what had happened and closed down their turntables. Reporters sent to Kensington Palace, where Diana had lived, and Buckingham Palace found hundreds and then thousands of people gathering in silence. There was nothing to see, or do, but they felt the need to be there. The royal family, including Prince Charles and the Princes William and Harry, were on holiday at Balmoral Castle. It was there that the first

rumblings of discontent with the reaction of the senior Royals began to be heard.

At 11 a.m. on the Sunday morning, six hours after the death of the princess had been confirmed, the royal family attended morning service at the small parish church in Crathie. By agreement with the Queen's staff, the service made no mention of Diana, although there was a prayer which included the words: 'We remember all those who at this time need to know your presence. All those whose lives are darkened by tragedy and grief.' However, the sermon, preached by a visiting clergyman from the Outer Hebrides, included several Billy Connolly jokes. The next cause of comment came when the Queen decided not to return to London. The Royal Standard only flies from Buckingham Palace when the Queen is in residence, so while the Queen stayed away there was no visible sign, such as a flag flying at half-mast, that the Royal family was in mourning. Questions were asked in the press, including one newspaper which, after several

days, carried the huge headline: 'WHERE ARE YOU MA'AM?'

Tony Blair's government, the masters of spin, became concerned about criticism of the Royal family and intervened, 'advising' the Palace on the best way to proceed. The Queen then returned to London and the Union flag was hoisted over Buckingham Palace, flying at half-mast. The Palace to which the Queen returned did not resemble the one she had left, for by now there was a massive carpet of floral tributes outside, with even more outside Kensington Palace. Public reaction on this scale to a royal death was unprecedented and it kept on growing. People travelled to London from all over the country and, interviewed on television and radio, they simply said that they 'just felt the need to be part of it'. The Queen, belatedly, broadcast to the nation on television and repaired much of the damage with what came across as a warm, heartfelt tribute to Diana. But criticism continued, not helped by a debate over whether or not Diana warranted a

The Prince of Wales,
Prince Harry, Earl Spencer,
Prince William and the
Duke of Edinburgh
follow the coffin as it
enters Westminster
Abbey.

state funeral. One problem here was that Diana had lost the title 'HRH' after the divorce, but the outcome was a state funeral in all but name. The public was clearly not interested in the niceties of protocol.

The funeral itself, in Westminster Abbey, was unique in British history, a mixture of religion and showbusiness. Elton John, a favourite of the princess, had been asked to sing and he spent the days before the funeral writing an updated version of 'Candle in the Wind', his tribute to the late Hollywood star Marilyn Monroe. John and his lyricist Bernie Taupin spent a frantic few days faxing new lyrics for the song between London and Hollywood. The resultant record was to become the biggest selling single in the history of the record industry. Tony Blair read one of the lessons at the funeral, but the most startling moment came when Earl Spencer rose to give the eulogy. Staring directly at the royal family across Diana's coffin he said that Diana 'needed no royal title to generate her particular brand of magic', a swipe at the decision to strip her of the title 'Her Royal Highness'. Addressing Princes William and Harry directly, he made the following promise to his dead sister: 'On behalf of your mother and sisters, I pledge that we, your blood family, will do all we can to continue the imaginative and loving way in which you were steering these two exceptional young men so that their souls are not simply immersed by duty and tradition, but can sing openly as you planned.' The speech, whatever one thought about the appropriateness of some of the content, was undoubtedly a *tour de force* and at the end of it

(Below) The funeral
became a huge
media event, with
camera cranes lifted
into place
above The Mall.

(Right) Thousands
of people gathered
in Hyde Park, where
the funeral service
was relayed on giant
screens.

the congregation in the Abbey and the vast crowd watching a relay of the service in Hyde Park broke into applause. The royal family sat in silence.

After the funeral, the hearse carried Diana to her last resting place, an island in a small lake at the family home of Althorp. The journey was covered by television cameras all the way to the gates of the estate and it was in a strange way the most moving part of the entire week. The controversies and the arguments could now be put aside. Hundreds of thousands of people lined the route from central London to the M1. Garlands of flowers were thrown on to the hearse and so many landed on the bonnet

that the driver had to stop on a slip road before the M1 to clear them away. The hearse left the motorway and drove through winding lanes to Althorp and in through the gates, which at once closed. The nation slowly returned to something approaching normal, perhaps feeling that the last words of Lord Spencer's oration served well enough as both a testament to his sister and an explanation of her extraordinary appeal: 'We give thanks for the life of a woman I am so proud to call my sister – the unique, the complex, the extraordinary and irreplaceable Diana, whose beauty, both internal and external, will never be extinguished from our minds.'

Sources and Bibliography

The sources for this book are necessarily diverse, ranging from the BBC archive to newspaper cuttings chronicling the events as they happened. Many books have been useful as background reading and where I have quoted from then they are given due recognition in the text. Readers interested in the subjects covered here may find some or all of the following books of interest:

Chronicle of the 20th Century, Longman.

A Social History of British Broadcasting, Paddy Scannell and David Cardiff, Basil Blackwell.

The General Strike of 1926: Its Origins and History, R Page Arnott, Augustus M Kelley.

Crashes: Why They Happen, What To Do, Robert Beckman, Sidgwick & Jackson.

The History of Broadcasting in the UK, Asa Briggs, OUP.

King Edward VIII, Philip Ziegler, Collins.

What Did You Do in the War, Auntie? Tom Hickman, BBC Books.

War Report: D-Day to VE Day, BBC Books.

BBC At War, Antonia White, BBC.

From Our Own Correspondent, Edited by Tony Grant, Pan.

Suez, Keith Kyle, Weidenfeld & Nicholson.

Cutting the Lion's Tale, Mohammed H Heikal, Andre Deutsch.

The Team That Wouldn't Die, John Roberts, Arthur Barker Ltd.

England's Glory, Dave Hill, Pan Books.

The Queen, Ben Pimlott, HarperCollins.

Elizabeth, Sarah Bradford, Heinemann.

Moon Shot, Alan Shepard and Deke Slayton, Virgin Books.

One Hundred Days, Admiral Sandy Woodward, HarperCollins.

The Falklands Conflict, Valerie Adams, Wayland.

One of Us, Hugo Young, Macmillan.

The Wall Falls, Cornelia Heins, Grey Seal Books.

Diana: One of the Family?, Paul James, Sidgwick & Jackson.

The Northern Ireland Question in British Politics, Edited by Peter Catterall and Sean McDougal, Macmillan.

CD Track Listing

The General Strike – 1926
Track 1: News bulletin about the general situation, including Cardinal Bourne's views, read by Sir Charles Carpendale.
Track 2: News bulletin quoting AJ Cook, the miners' leader, read by Sir Charles Carpendale.
Track 3: News bulletin about milk churns in Hyde Park, read by Lance Sieveking.
Track 4: News bulletin announcing that the strike is over, read by Sir Charles Carpendale.
Track 5: 'Jerusalem' read by Sir John Reith. (Re-recorded for the National Programme 14/5/32).

The Wall Street Crash – 1929
Track 6: Wall Street humour from the US comedian Eddie Cantor.
Track 7: Newsreel commentary describing the scene outside the Wall Street Stock Exchange.
Track 8: An unknown trader recalls the panic and feelings of failure.
Track 9: An unknown investor recalls being 'wiped out'.

The Abdication of Edward VIII – 1936
Track 10: Edward VII announces his abdication. Introduction by Sir John Reith, 11/12/36.

The Declaration of War – 1939
Track 11: Neville Chamberlain announces that the country is at war, 3/9/39.
Track 12: Winston Churchill's 'finest hour' speech, 18/6/40.
Track 13: A bomb falls on Broadcasting House. News bulletin read by Bruce Belfrage, 15/10/40.
Track 14: News bulleting about the advance at El Alamein, read by Bruce Belfrage, 4/11/42
Track 15: Live battlefield reports by Frank Gillard in Normandy, 14/8/44 and Stanley Maxted in Arnhem, 20/9/44. Live report from Belsen by Richard Dimbleby, 17/4/45.
Track 16: News bulletin with details of the dropping of the Atomic bomb, read by Frank Phillips, 6/8/45.

The King is Dead. Long Live the Queen – 1952
Track 17: Death of George VI. News announcement by John Snagge, 6/5/52.
Track 18: Report from Frank Gillard in Kenya as the Queen is given the news of her father's death, 6/2/52
Track 19: The lying in state of George VI, report given by Richard Dimbleby, 12/2/52. The Coronation of Elizabeth II, a report by John Snagge, 2/6/53.

The Suez Crisis – 1956
Track 20: Prime Ministerial broadcast to the nation, by Sir Anthony Eden, 3/11/56
Track 21: Opposition broadcast asking for the Prime Minister to resign, by Hugh Gaitskell, 4/11/56
Track 22: Trafalgar Square speech attacking the government's policy on Egypt, by Aneurin Bevan, 4/11/56.
Track 23: Announcement of the ceasefire in Parliament, 6/11/56.

The Munich Air Crash – 1958
Track 24: Announcement of the Munich air crash. News bulletin by Kenneth Kendall, 6/2/58.
Track 25: Interview with journalist Geoffrey Green, 8/2/58.
Track 26: Survivor Harry Gregg describes the crash, 8/2/58.
Track 27: Sir Matt Busby records a message from his hospital bed in Munich to be played to the crowd at Old Trafford, 8/3/58.

The Assassination of President Kennedy – 1963
Track 28: President Kennedy broadcasts to the nation about Russian missiles in Cuba, 22/10/62.
Track 29: First announcement of the shooting. Radio Newsreel bulletin, 22/11/63.
Track 30: Announcement of the death of the president. Home Service news bulletin, 22/11/63.
Track 31: Announcement of the shooting by conductor Erich Leinsdorf at a lunchtime concert in Boston, 22/11/63.

England Win the World Cup – 1966
Track 32: Interview with American tourists in Carnaby Street, 13/9/67.
Track 33: An extract from Kenneth Wolstenholme's match commentary from the 1966 World Cup final, 30/7/66.

Men on the Moon – 1969
Track 34: 'The Eagle has landed'. Commentary by Neil Armstrong, Buzz Aldrin, Michael Collins and staff at NASA, 20/7/69.
Track 35: 'One small step for man, one giant leap for mankind'. Commentary by Neil Armstrong, 21/7/69.

The Munich Olympics – 1972
Track 36: Announcement of the attack. News bulletin, 5/9/72.
Track 37: A German government spokesman tells the story of the failed rescue attempt, 6/9/72.
Track 38: IOC President Avery Brundage speaks at a memorial service in the Olympic Stadium, Munich, 6/9/72.

The Birth of the First Test Tube Baby – 1978
Track 39: Dr Patrick Steptoe talks through the birth of Louise Brown, 23/8/78.

The Murder of John Lennon – 1980
Track 40: Announcement of the shooting by Christopher Slade. News bulletin, 9/12/80.
Track 41: Account of the shooting by eyewitness Dr Steven Lynn, 9/12/80.

The Falklands War – 1982
Track 42: 'I counted them all out…' News report on a British air raid on Port Stanley, by Brian Hanrahan, 1/5/82.
Track 43: MOD spokesman Ian McDonald gives the first news of the attack on HMS Sheffield. News report, 4/5/82.
Track 44: Details of the attack on HMS Sheffield. Report by Brian Hanrahan, 5/5/82.

The Brighton Bombing – 1984
Track 45: News report by John Timpson. Interview with a shocked Mrs Thatcher by John Cole. 12/10/84.

The Lockerbie Disaster – 1988
Track 46: First announcement of the disaster. From The World Tonight on Radio 4 read by Alexander MacLeod, 21/12/88.
Track 47: Eyewitness account by Peter O'Brien, 22/12/88.
Track 48: Confirmation of the bomb. News report read by Mick Charles, 28/12/88.

The Berlin Wall Comes Down – 1989
Track 49: Commentary on the first 'official' breach in the wall. News report by Graham Leach, 11/11/89.

The Resignation of Margaret Thatcher – 1990
Track 50: Mrs Thatcher speaks on the Conservative Party leadership election, 19/11/90.
Track 51: James Naughtie reports on the first ballot. News bulletin, 20/11/90.
Track 52: Mrs Thatcher vows to fight on, 21/11/90.
Track 53: Announcement of Mrs Thatcher's resignation. News bulletin read by Peter Donaldson, 22/11/90.
Track 54: Mrs Thatcher says goodbye to No.10 Downing Street, 28/11/90.

The Dunblane Massacre – 1996
Track 55: First announcement of the attack. News bulletin on Radio 5 by Stephen Sackur and Diana Madill, 13/3/96.
Track 56: More news of the attack. News report read by Reeval Alderson, 13/3/96.
Track 57: The death toll is reported by Police Superintendent Lewis Munn, 13/3/96.
Track 58: 'Evil visited us yesterday…' Interview with Ron Taylor, headmaster of Dunblane School, 14/3/96.

The Death of Diana, Princess of Wales – 1997
Track 59: First announcement of the crash. News report read by Gail Downey, 31/8/97.
Track 60: Unnofficial announcement of Diana's death. News report from Up All Night on Radio 5 presented by Richard Dallyn and Paul Reynolds, 31/8/97.
Track 61: Official announcement of Diana's death. Special radio programme presented by James Naughtie and Andrew Crawford, 31/8/97.
Track 62: The Prime Minister, Tony Blair, describes Diana as the 'People's Princess', 31/8/97.

Track 31: excerpt from Erich Leinsdorf's speech regarding the assassination of President Kennedy in 1963, courtesy of BMG Entertainment International UK & Ireland Ltd.
Track 39: courtesy of Film Images.
The Publishers have made every effort to trace copyright holders of material reproduced in this book and accompanying CD. If, however, they have inadvertently made any error, they would be grateful for any notification.

Index